Essentials of
Nonprofit Fundraising

Steven M. Bragg

AccountingTools®

For more information about AccountingTools® products, visit our Web site at www.accountingtools.com.

Table of Contents

Table of Contents

About the Author

Steven Bragg, CPA, has been the chief financial officer or controller of four companies, as well as a consulting manager at Ernst & Young. He received a master's degree in finance from Bentley College, an MBA from Babson College, and a Bachelor's degree in Economics from the University of Maine. He has been a two-time president of the Colorado Mountain Club, and is an avid alpine skier, mountain biker, and certified master diver. Mr. Bragg resides in Centennial, Colorado. He has written more than 300 books and courses, including *New Controller Guidebook*, *GAAP Guidebook*, and *Payroll Management*.

Steven maintains the accountingtools.com web site, which contains continuing professional education courses, the Accounting Best Practices podcast, and thousands of articles on accounting subjects.

Buy Additional AccountingTools Courses

AccountingTools offers more than 1,500 hours of CPE courses, with concentrations in accounting, auditing, finance, taxation, and ethics. Related courses that you might like include:

- Auditing Nonprofit Entities
- Nonprofit Accounting

Go to accountingtools.com/cpe to view these additional courses.

AccountingTools®

Chapter 1
Overview of Nonprofit Fundraising

Introduction

Few nonprofit organizations can generate sufficient cash from their own operations to support themselves. In most cases, it is essential for these entities to engage in ongoing *fundraising* activities – which is defined as the generation of revenue for charitable purposes. The need to conduct successful fundraising operations is usually so critical that a nonprofit will fail if it cannot cost-effectively raise funds from a variety of sources. Therefore, this book is targeted at the most essential of all nonprofit activities – fundraising. In the following chapters, we cover every aspect of fundraising, including donor behavior, fundraising planning, and donor retention. But first, we will provide a brief overview of the types of fundraising in which nonprofits engage, and the guiding principles that they follow in their fundraising activities.

Fundraising Classifications

Nonprofit organizations typically focus their fundraising efforts within specific classifications. Here are the more common categories:

- *Annual fund.* This is a fundraising campaign that is intended to raise unrestricted funds on an annual basis. These funds are typically used to support an organization's ongoing operations, programs, scholarships, staff salaries, facility maintenance, and so forth. These campaigns are usually targeted at a broad donor base, where donations of all sizes are encouraged. A key component of these campaigns is to build participation among donors over the long term. Many organizations use the annual fund as a foundation for larger fundraising efforts, such as capital campaigns or endowment growth.
- *Capital campaign.* This is a large-scale, time-limited fundraising campaign to raise a large amount of money for a specific project, such as constructing a new building, renovating facilities, purchasing major equipment, or growing an endowment. Capital campaigns typically involve securing large donations from major donors, foundations, and corporations before seeking broader public contributions. Having a lead donation in hand makes it much easier to attract additional donors.
- *Corporate contributions.* Corporate support for a nonprofit provides vital funding and resources, enabling the organization to expand its impact and reach. It also lends credibility and visibility, attracting additional donors and partners. In return, companies benefit from enhanced reputation, employee engagement, and alignment with corporate social responsibility goals. This synergy helps both entities achieve their missions more effectively.
- *Government grants.* Government grants provide crucial funding for nonprofits to support their programs and services without the pressure of repayment.

They enable organizations to expand their impact, reach underserved communities, and address specific societal challenges. Additionally, securing a government grant can enhance a nonprofit's credibility, attracting further donations and partnerships. However, these grants often come with strict compliance and reporting requirements.

- *Planned giving.* This is a philanthropic strategy that allows individuals to make charitable contributions through financial or estate planning. These gifts are typically arranged during a donor's lifetime but are not realized by the nonprofit until a later date, often after the donor's passing. Planned giving provides long-term financial support for nonprofits while offering potential tax benefits and legacy opportunities for donors. However, donors tend to be quite specific about how their contributions are to be used, so these funds may not be available to support the ongoing operational needs of a nonprofit.

- *Endowment campaign.* This is a strategic fundraising initiative aimed at building a nonprofit's endowment fund, which is a permanent financial asset that is designed to provide long-term stability and sustainability. The principal of the endowment is typically invested, and the nonprofit uses a portion of the investment earnings (rather than the principal) to support its programs, operations, or specific initiatives.

> **Note:** Many larger nonprofits run endowment campaigns continually. By doing so, they hope to eventually build up such large endowments that the resulting investment income is hefty enough to minimize the need for an annual fund.

EXAMPLE

The "Unlocking Bright Futures" annual fund campaign is a year-long initiative to raise $250,000 to support scholarships, tutoring programs, and school supplies for low-income students. This campaign engages donors of all levels, from first-time contributors to major gift supporters, ensuring every child has access to the education they deserve.

EXAMPLE

A local hospital launches a $10 million capital campaign to build a new cancer treatment center. The hospital initially secures $6 million from major donors. It then hosts fundraising galas, promotes donation opportunities on social media, and encourages community giving. After successfully raising the full amount, the hospital begins construction, keeps donors updated on progress, and holds a ribbon-cutting ceremony to celebrate their contributions.

EXAMPLE

The Legacy of Hope planned giving campaign encourages donors to leave a lasting impact by including the City Gardens nonprofit in their wills, trusts, or estate plans. The campaign highlights how planned gifts sustain the organization's mission for future generations. The goal of the campaign is to secure at least 20 new legacy society members in the first year, and generate $500,000 in pledged planned gifts over five years.

EXAMPLE

The Forest Rebuilding Trust has launched the *Securing Our Future* endowment campaign to ensure long-term financial sustainability and expand its impact for generations to come. The organization's goal is to raise $5 million to establish a permanent fund that will generate reliable income to support its programs, staff, and community initiatives in perpetuity. The goal of the campaign is to obtain $5 million over the next three years, with the funds being invested to generate an annual return of 5%. This should provide the organization with a sustainable income of $250,000 per year to support its mission.

Tip: Many nonprofits set up their annual fund campaigns to encourage automated monthly deductions from donor bank accounts, or via credit card charges. Either approach can result in more total payments than would be made through a single annual payment, since donors do not feel the pain of a single, large payment. Also, these payments tend to be self-perpetuating, with no additional fundraising contacts needed unless a donor cancels a payment or the person's credit card expires.

Donors are rarely interested in donating funds to a specific campaign. Instead, they are more interested in putting funds into areas where the money will make the most difference. Consequently, the best fundraising approach is to focus on the needs of the individual donor, and set them up with whichever fundraising classification makes the most sense from the perspective of their personal needs.

Individuals typically closely associate with their giving, and so rarely give significant amounts to causes outside of the areas with which they have a strong connection. For example, an individual who closely associates with ballet might donate a significant proportion of her income to the local ballet company, without feeling any particular need to donate to other causes outside of the dance area.

Fundraising Principles

There are several core principles that can be used by nonprofits to maximize the amount of funds obtained within the shortest amount of time. They are as follows:

- *Concentrated time period.* Compress the duration of a fundraising campaign in order to convince businesspeople to assist with the effort. When they are only faced with a short-duration campaign, they are more likely to provide assistance. A further advantage of conducting a short-term campaign is that it can appear repeatedly in the news cycle over a short period of time, thereby improving the public recognition of the campaign.
- *Obtain a pace-setting gift.* Find a donor early in the campaign who is willing to pay a substantial portion of the entire fundraising amount, but only if the full amount is raised by a specific date. This provides a solid reason for donors to contribute to the campaign within the designated time period.
- *Engage in targeted outreach.* Focus on specific donor segments that are most likely to contribute, such as past donors or individuals with a known interest

in your cause. Tailored messaging and personalized appeals can significantly increase response rates and funding.

- *Use compelling storytelling.* Share impactful stories that highlight the problem, your solution, and the tangible results of donations. Emotional connections motivate donors to give quickly and generously.
- *Leverage digital channels.* Utilize email marketing, social media, and crowdfunding platforms to reach a broader audience quickly. Paid ads and search engine optimization can amplify visibility and attract more donations rapidly.
- *Use corporate partnerships.* Collaborate with businesses for matching gift programs, sponsorships, or cause marketing campaigns. Corporate support can significantly boost funds within a short timeframe through access to their networks and resources.
- *Encourage peer-to-peer fundraising.* Empower supporters to raise funds on your behalf by providing easy-to-use tools and resources. This approach expands your reach exponentially through personal networks.
- *Use a data-driven strategy.* Analyze donor behavior and past campaign performance to refine targeting and messaging. A strategic approach based on data can enhance efficiency and maximize funding quickly.

We will discuss these principles at greater length in the following chapters.

The Fundraising Staff

Having a dedicated fundraising staff is crucial for a nonprofit entity, as it brings specialized skills and focus to securing the financial resources needed to sustain and expand its mission. Trained fundraising professionals can develop and execute comprehensive strategies, build relationships with donors, write effective grant proposals, and manage fundraising events with expertise. Their ability to analyze donor data and trends also enables more targeted and successful campaigns. Moreover, a dedicated team allows program staff to concentrate on delivering services without being stretched thin by funding responsibilities. However, hiring specialized fundraising staff can be costly, which poses a challenge for smaller nonprofits with limited budgets. There is also a risk of becoming overly reliant on a few individuals for funding success, potentially leading to disruptions if they leave. Balancing the costs and benefits is essential, but for many nonprofits, the investment in dedicated fundraising staff is justified by the increased efficiency and revenue they can generate.

The Certified Fund Raising Professional

A Certified Fund Raising Executive (CFRE) is a professional who has earned the CFRE credential, which is a globally recognized certification for fundraising professionals. The CFRE designation demonstrates a fundraiser's commitment to ethical standards, expertise, and leadership in the nonprofit sector.

The key aspects of this certification are as follows:

- *Eligibility requirements*. The certification requires a minimum number of years of experience in fundraising, proven success in securing charitable contributions, a combination of professional education and volunteer service, and a commitment to ethical best practices in fundraising.
- *Examination*. Candidates must pass an exam covering key areas like donor stewardship, prospect research, ethics, leadership, and fundraising techniques.
- *Ethical requirements*. CFRE holders adhere to the Donor Bill of Rights and the Code of Ethical Standards set by the Association of Fundraising Professionals (AFP) and other governing bodies (we discuss fundraising ethics in the next chapter).
- *Renewal requirement*. Certification must be renewed every three years through ongoing continued education training and professional practice.

Many fundraising professionals in the nonprofit sector obtain the CFRE in order to increase their earning potential and job prospects. Having this certificate also strengthens trust with donors, organizations, and the public.

The Need for Fundraiser Retention

Raising funds is the engine that drives nonprofit operations, so it would make sense to focus intensively on reducing turnover among nonprofit fundraisers. Donors are more likely to continue contributing money for extended periods of time when they have built up relations with fundraising personnel at their chosen charities. Despite this obvious reason to retain fundraisers, most nonprofits have great difficulty in doing so. Depending on the research source, it appears that most fundraisers only stay in the position for somewhere in the range of 14 to 24 months. Whenever there is turnover in one of these positions, it becomes much more likely that donors will shrink the size of their donations, delay them, or cut them off entirely. Thus, it is critical to hold onto fundraisers. How can this be done?

The first step is understanding why fundraisers leave. There are several common reasons for doing so, which include the following:

- *No career path*. Many fundraisers are brought in specifically for that role, with no opportunity to advance into a management role.
- *Lack of credit*. It requires a substantial amount of work to raise money, and yet fundraisers may find that the credit for their work is spread across the entire team, or even hogged by the administrator of the nonprofit. Worse yet, fundraisers may be blamed for a lack of funds brought in, even though the underlying reason is the lack of resources provided by the administrator.
- *Conflicts over how to raise money*. Management may have specific ideas regarding the best way to raise money from donors, and will mandate that this approach be followed. Fundraisers may come into the position with

alternative views, and so leave in frustration when they are not allowed to pursue their own approaches.

- *Lack of support.* Nonprofit managers do not provide sufficient support to their fundraisers, resulting in lost fundraising opportunities or excessive overtime work by the fundraisers.

Clearly, taking the reverse of the preceding issues will lengthen fundraiser employment periods, and thereby increase the amount of funds raised. This means offering fundraisers a meaningful career path, giving credit when it is due, valuing the opinions of fundraisers, and giving them enough support to accomplish their fundraising targets.

Summary

This chapter discussed the importance of retaining fundraising professionals within nonprofit organizations, highlighting that turnover among fundraisers can significantly impact donations and overall nonprofit operations. It also explained several common reasons why fundraisers leave their positions. To mitigate these issues and retain fundraisers longer, we suggested providing a meaningful career path, recognizing fundraisers' contributions, respecting their fundraising approaches, and offering adequate support. This strategic approach can enhance fundraiser retention and ultimately increase the funds raised for nonprofit endeavors.

Chapter 2
Fundraising Ethics

Introduction

A number of ethical considerations can arise when a nonprofit engages in fundraising activities. There are several schools of thought regarding how to resolve these ethical situations, but we prefer to address the topic by using a number of case studies that are routinely encountered within the industry, and pose questions that should be resolved when deciding upon the best course of action. The bulk of this chapter is comprised of case studies.

Does the Public Have a Right to be Excluded from Donation Requests?

Sarah is a retired teacher who donates occasionally to causes she cares about. A few years ago, she made a one-time donation to Helping Hands Foundation, a nonprofit that provides food assistance to low-income families. Since then, she has received frequent donation requests via mail, email, and phone calls from Helping Hands and other nonprofits that may have purchased or shared donor lists.

The Ethical Dilemma

Sarah finds the constant requests intrusive and overwhelming. She has asked Helping Hands to remove her from their contact list, but she still receives occasional requests. She also gets donation appeals from other organizations she never supported, likely due to donor list-sharing practices.

Feeling frustrated, Sarah believes that individuals should have the right to opt out of donation solicitations, just like they can opt out of telemarketing calls or promotional emails. However, nonprofits argue that fundraising is essential to their survival, and reaching out to potential donors—including past supporters—is a standard and necessary practice.

Ethical Considerations

The situation raises the following ethical questions:

- The Right to Privacy vs. the Needs of Nonprofits

  o Does Sarah (and the public) have the right to be free from donation requests?
  o Do nonprofits have the right to contact previous or potential donors as part of their fundraising efforts?

- Informed Consent and Transparency

  o Should nonprofits be required to get explicit opt-in consent before sending donation requests?
  o Is it ethical for organizations to share or sell donor lists without clear disclosure?

- Donor Fatigue and Public Perception

  o Could excessive fundraising appeals lead to frustration and decreased trust in the nonprofit sector?
  o How can nonprofits balance effective fundraising with respect for donor preferences?

- Legal & Ethical Obligations

  o Some countries and states have "Do Not Call" or "Do Not Mail" registries for marketing—should nonprofits be required to follow similar rules?
  o Is it ethical to make opting out difficult (e.g., requiring mailed requests to be removed from a list)?

Conclusion

Nonprofits rely on fundraising to fulfill their missions, but they must also respect donor privacy and preferences. Striking a balance between effective donor outreach and ethical transparency is key to maintaining public trust and long-term support.

Should a Fundraiser Use Guilt to Secure a Donation?

Emma is a fundraising officer at Hope Haven, a nonprofit that provides housing assistance to low-income families. The organization is facing a financial shortfall and urgently needs to raise $250,000 to keep several families from eviction. Emma has a meeting with Mr. Davis, a longtime donor who has given modestly in the past. She knows that he has the financial capacity to make a major gift, but he has not increased his giving in recent years.

The Ethical Dilemma

During their conversation, Emma shares stories of families who will lose their homes if funding is not secured. She considers using a guilt-based appeal to persuade Mr. Davis to make a larger contribution. She is debating between two approaches:

- Empathy-Driven Appeal:

  o Emma tells Mr. Davis about the challenges families face and how his support can make a difference.
  o She frames the donation as a positive opportunity to help rather than an obligation.
  o She ensures Mr. Davis understands that all gifts, regardless of size, are appreciated.

- Guilt-Driven Appeal:
  - Emma highlights Mr. Davis's financial privilege and asks if he can live with himself knowing that families might become homeless while he has the means to help.
  - She suggests that by not giving more, he is part of the problem.
  - She uses emotionally charged language to make Mr. Davis feel personally responsible.

Emma is torn. The guilt-driven approach could motivate Mr. Davis to make a substantial gift, potentially helping more families. However, it might also make him uncomfortable, damage their relationship, or make him feel coerced rather than inspired.

Ethical Considerations

The fundraiser should have respect for a donor's autonomy. This means that it is better to encourage donors to give voluntarily, rather than pressuring them to do so. By encouraging voluntary giving, it is easier to build long-term relationships with donors, which emphasizes larger donations over the long-term than over the short-term. The main concern with the use of guilt-based appeals is that it leads to donor fatigue or resentment, which may eventually drive the donor away.

Conclusion

Fundraisers have a duty to uphold ethical standards while maximizing support for their mission. Using guilt may yield short-term financial gains, but could damage donor relationships and undermine trust in the long run. Instead, focusing on inspiration, transparency, and donor empowerment is more ethical and sustainable.

Should a Nonprofit Conduct Ethical Screenings of Donors?

Bright Futures Foundation (BFF) is a nonprofit that provides scholarships to underprivileged students. Recently, BFF received an unexpected $5 million donation from Mr. Carter, a wealthy businessman. The gift could fully fund scholarships for hundreds of students over the next five years.

However, after the donation was made public, concerns arose about Mr. Carter's business practices. Investigative reports revealed that his company has been involved in environmental violations and labor rights abuses overseas. Some of BFF's stakeholders—including students, staff, and existing donors—question whether the organization should accept the donation from a controversial source.

BFF does not currently have an ethical screening policy for donors, but this situation has sparked debate over whether they should establish one.

The Ethical Dilemma

BFF must decide whether to:

- Accept the donation, reasoning that the funds will directly benefit students, regardless of the donor's past actions.
- Reject the donation, maintaining the nonprofit's ethical integrity but potentially losing a transformative funding opportunity.
- Implement an ethical donor screening policy, ensuring future donations align with BFF's values—but potentially reducing fundraising opportunities.

Ethical Considerations

- Mission Integrity vs. Financial Necessity

  o Would accepting the donation compromise BFF's mission and values?
  o Does the impact of the funds outweigh concerns about the donor's ethics?

- Public Perception and Trust

  o If the public sees BFF accepting money from a controversial source, could it damage trust in the nonprofit?
  o Could rejecting the gift discourage other major donors from contributing?

- Accountability for Donor Actions

  o Is BFF responsible for where the money comes from, or only for how it is used?
  o Should nonprofits accept "tainted money" if it funds positive work?

- Ethical Consistency

  o If BFF accepts this donation, would it set a precedent for accepting future donations from ethically questionable sources?
  o If they reject it, how will they determine which donors meet ethical standards in the future?

- Impact on Beneficiaries

  o If the donation is rejected, students who would have received scholarships may lose opportunities.
  o Is it ethical to prioritize moral purity over immediate aid to those in need?

Conclusion

BFF faces a difficult choice between financial sustainability and ethical integrity. Implementing an ethical donor screening policy could help prevent future dilemmas, but it may also limit fundraising potential. The decision ultimately depends on whether the organization prioritizes immediate impact or long-term ethical alignment.

Should a Nonprofit Prioritize Wealthy Donors Over Grassroots Supporters?

Community First Initiative (CFI) is a nonprofit that advocates for affordable housing policies and provides direct assistance to low-income families. CFI has traditionally relied on grassroots donations from community members, many of whom are directly affected by housing challenges. However, these smaller donations are unpredictable, making it difficult to sustain long-term projects.

Recently, CFI has attracted the attention of wealthy philanthropists and corporate donors who are willing to contribute large sums of money. However, some of these major donors have different priorities than the grassroots supporters. Some funders prefer policy solutions that align with their business interests, while grassroots supporters tend to favor direct services like rental assistance and eviction prevention. As CFI considers its fundraising strategy, it faces a critical ethical dilemma:

- Prioritizing Major Donors – Accepting large gifts would provide financial stability and allow CFI to expand its programs, but it may shift decision-making power away from the community. Wealthy donors could have an outsized influence on the organization's priorities.
- Prioritizing Grassroots Supporters – Keeping the focus on smaller, community-driven donations ensures that those most affected by housing issues have a strong voice in the nonprofit's direction. However, this approach may result in financial instability and limit the organization's growth.

The Ethical Dilemma

CFI's leadership must decide:

- Should they focus on cultivating relationships with major donors, even if it means adjusting their programs to align with funders' interests?
- Or should they continue prioritizing grassroots fundraising, even if it means slower growth and fewer resources?

Ethical Considerations

- Power and Representation
  - If major donors contribute most of the funding, do they have a right to influence the nonprofit's priorities?
  - How can CFI ensure that grassroots voices remain central in decision-making?
- Mission Integrity
  - Would shifting priorities to appeal to wealthy donors compromise the organization's original mission?
  - Should a nonprofit ever adjust its programs based on donor preferences?
- Financial Sustainability vs. Democratic Governance

- o Is it ethical to prioritize financial security over community representation?
- o Could relying too much on grassroots donations limit the organization's impact?

- Public Perception & Trust

  - o Would grassroots supporters feel betrayed if the nonprofit starts prioritizing the interests of the wealthy?
  - o How could CFI maintain transparency in its decision-making to preserve trust?

Conclusion

CFI must carefully navigate the tension between funding stability and community representation. While major donors can provide financial security, prioritizing them too much could dilute grassroots voices. An ethical approach would involve transparency, donor diversity, and a commitment to mission integrity.

Should Donor Money be Spent on Fundraising?

Bright Futures Foundation is a nonprofit dedicated to providing scholarships for underprivileged students. Recently, the organization received a $500,000 major gift from a generous donor, Mrs. Thompson, who expressed a desire to help as many students as possible.

The executive team is considering using $100,000 of this donation to invest in a fundraising campaign that could attract even more donors and significantly increase future scholarship funding. However, the donor was not explicitly told that a portion of her gift might be used for fundraising rather than direct scholarships.

The Ethical Dilemma

The nonprofit faces a difficult decision, which is as follows:

- Use 100% of Mrs. Thompson's donation for scholarships, honoring what she likely assumed would happen but missing an opportunity to grow funding.
- Allocate $100,000 to fundraising efforts, which could result in much more money for scholarships in the future but may raise ethical concerns about donor expectations and transparency.

The leadership team believes that investing in fundraising will ultimately benefit more students, but they also worry about the ethical implications of not explicitly informing Mrs. Thompson that part of her donation will be used in this manner.

Ethical Considerations

- Donor Intent and Transparency:

  o Did Mrs. Thompson expect her entire gift to go directly to scholarships?

  o Should the nonprofit have communicated that some of the donation might be reinvested in fundraising?

- Impact on Beneficiaries:

  o If the investment in fundraising leads to more donations, more students will receive scholarships.

  o However, in the short term, fewer students will benefit from Mrs. Thompson's donation.

- Sustainability & Stewardship:

  o Investing in fundraising could ensure long-term sustainability and help more people over time.

  o But does using donor money for fundraising align with the nonprofit's ethical responsibility to maximize immediate impact?

- Public Trust & Perception:

  o Would donors feel deceived if they learned their gift was used for fundraising?

  o How might this decision affect donor trust and future giving?

Conclusion

In short, nonprofits must balance immediate needs with sustainable growth while ensuring that donors feel their contributions are being used ethically and effectively.

Should a Nonprofit Pay its Fundraisers a Percentage of the Funds Raised?

Hope for All (HFA) is a nonprofit that provides medical care to underserved communities. To expand its impact, HFA needs to raise $2 million over the next year. The board is considering offering its fundraising team a commission-based compensation structure, where fundraisers earn a percentage of the total funds they secure.

Some board members argue that this will motivate fundraisers to work harder and ultimately increase donations. However, others worry that this model could create ethical concerns, including donor exploitation, conflicts of interest, and financial transparency issues.

The Ethical Dilemma

HFA must decide whether to implement a commission-based compensation structure for its fundraising team. It is considering paying fundraisers a percentage of the funds raised. This approach could incentivize fundraisers to be more aggressive and effective, and might also lead to higher overall donations. However, it could also lead to pressure tactics, donor manipulation, or unethical solicitation practices. This approach might also create a conflict of interest, as fundraisers could prioritize high-net-worth donors over long-term donor relationships. And finally, it violates industry best practices—organizations like CFRE International and the Association of Fundraising Professionals (AFP) oppose commission-based pay in nonprofits.

Ethical Considerations

- Donor Trust and Transparency

  o Would donors still give if they knew a portion of their gift was going directly to a fundraiser's commission?
  o Does commission-based pay violate donor intent, since donors typically expect their contributions to support programs, not individual salaries?

- Risk of Unethical Fundraising Practices

  o Could commission-based pay lead to pressure tactics, misleading appeals, or aggressive solicitation?
  o Might fundraisers prioritize large donors over small, long-term supporters to maximize their earnings?

- Industry Standards and Reputation

  o Organizations like AFP, CFRE International, and the Better Business Bureau Wise Giving Alliance strongly discourage commission-based pay in nonprofit fundraising.
  o Would adopting a commission model damage HFA's credibility in the nonprofit sector?

- Mission Alignment and Employee Ethics

  o Should a nonprofit's compensation model reflect its core values of service and integrity?
  o Could commission-based pay attract fundraisers who prioritize personal financial gain over ethical donor stewardship?

Conclusion

While commission-based pay may increase short-term fundraising success, it raises serious ethical concerns about donor trust, pressure tactics, and conflicts of interest. Nonprofits should explore alternative incentive structures that align with industry best practices while ensuring ethical and sustainable fundraising.

Should a Nonprofit Sell or Share its Donor Lists?

Helping Hands Foundation (HHF) is a nonprofit that provides food assistance to low-income families. Like many nonprofits, HHF relies heavily on donor contributions to fund its programs. Recently, HHF was approached by a marketing firm that works with other charities. The firm offered to purchase HHF's donor list for $50,000, with the promise that donors would only be contacted by "mission-aligned" organizations. Additionally, some of HHF's corporate partners have asked for access to the list in exchange for larger sponsorships. HHF's leadership team is considering the offer because:

- The money could directly support their programs.
- Some organizations that receive the list may also be doing good work.
- Many for-profit companies sell customer data—is this different?

However, the following concerns have also been raised:

- Many donors may not have agreed to have their information shared.
- If donors find out, they may feel betrayed and stop supporting HHF.
- Is sharing donor information without explicit consent appropriate?

The Ethical Dilemma

HHF must decide whether to:

- Sell the donor list, generating immediate funds but risking donor trust and privacy concerns.
- Share the list selectively, only with partner organizations that align with HHF's mission.
- Refuse to sell or share donor information, upholding strict privacy standards but missing out on financial support.

Ethical Considerations

- Donor Privacy and Consent

  o Did donors explicitly consent to having their information shared?
  o Would they feel betrayed if they started receiving unexpected solicitations?

- Trust and Reputation

  o Would selling donor data damage HHF's credibility and long-term donor relationships?
  o If donors lose trust, could it result in lower future donations?

- Transparency and Disclosure

  o Is HHF clearly informing donors how their data will be used?
  o Would adding an opt-in or opt-out policy for data sharing make this ethical?

- Mission and Financial Need

  o Would the funds raised from selling the list significantly benefit HHF's programs?
  o Does financial sustainability justify a potential ethical compromise?

- Legal and Industry Standards
  - Are there laws or nonprofit best practices regarding donor data protection?
  - Should nonprofits follow stricter ethical standards than for-profit companies?

Conclusion

While selling or sharing donor lists may provide financial benefits, it risks violating donor trust and privacy. Ethical best practices suggest that nonprofits should prioritize transparency and donor consent over short-term financial gain.

Summary

Ethical fundraising is about more than raising money—it is about doing so in a way that aligns with integrity, transparency, and respect for both donors and beneficiaries. Nonprofits must balance financial sustainability with ethical responsibility to maintain long-term trust and impact. This means making ethical decisions from the perspectives of donors and beneficiaries, where the interests of the nonprofit generally come in second. The result is usually a more satisfied group of partners that are more interested in doing business with the nonprofit over the long term.

For more specific guidelines regarding what to do in ethical situations, see the Code of Ethical Standards that is promulgated by the Association of Fundraising Professionals.

Chapter 3
Donor Behavior

Introduction

Charitable giving is a complex and multifaceted behavior influenced by various demographic and psychological factors. This chapter explores the characteristics of individual donors, examining how variables such as sex, ethnicity, age, and income shape donation patterns. Understanding these differences allows nonprofits to develop targeted fundraising strategies that align with donor motivations. Additionally, the chapter delves into the role of self-interest, empathy, social influence, and identity in philanthropy, shedding light on why people give and how they assess the utility of their donations. By analyzing these factors, organizations can foster deeper donor engagement and enhance the effectiveness of their fundraising efforts.

Donor Characteristics

Individual donors play a crucial role in charitable giving, and their donation behavior is influenced by several demographic factors, including sex, ethnicity, age, and income. These characteristics affect how much people give, the causes they support, and their motivations for donating.

General Characteristics of Individual Donors

Individual donors often exhibit a standard set of traits, which include the following:

- *Social responsibility.* Many donors give because they feel a moral obligation to help others or support causes they believe in.
- *Religious or cultural influences.* Faith-based traditions and cultural values often drive charitable giving.
- *Personal connection to a cause.* Individuals who have experienced or witnessed a specific issue (e.g., cancer, poverty, or education struggles) are more likely to donate to related organizations.
- *Tax benefits and incentives.* Some donors contribute for financial reasons, such as tax deductions.
- *Trust and transparency.* People are more likely to donate to organizations they perceive as trustworthy and efficient.

While these characteristics are widespread, donation behavior varies significantly based on sex, ethnicity, age, and income. We cover these variations in the following sub-topics.

Donation Characteristics by Demographics

There are significant differences in the donation patterns of donors, based on their genders, ethnicities, ages, and incomes.

Gender Differences in Giving

Men and women often differ in their giving patterns in the following ways:

- Women:
    - More likely to donate than men.
    - Tend to give smaller amounts but to a larger number of causes.
    - More inclined to support social services, education, health, and human rights organizations.
    - Prefer relational and community-based giving, valuing the personal impact of donations.

- Men:
    - More likely to donate larger amounts but to fewer causes.
    - Often support political, economic, and research-oriented causes.
    - More likely to be influenced by financial incentives, such as tax benefits.
    - Show a higher likelihood of contributing to legacy or endowment funds.

Ethnic and Racial Differences in Giving

Cultural backgrounds and community traditions shape donation behaviors in the following ways:

- White Donors:
    - Tend to give the largest amounts overall due to higher average income levels.
    - Support a broad range of causes, including education, arts, and health organizations.

- Black/African American Donors:
    - High participation in charitable giving, especially within faith-based organizations.
    - Strong traditions of communal support and grassroots philanthropy.
    - Often prioritize causes related to social justice, education, and community development.

- Hispanic/Latino Donors:
    - Giving is often tied to religious institutions and local community causes.
    - Higher likelihood of engaging in informal philanthropy (helping family members, crowdfunding, mutual aid).
    - Education and immigration-related causes are common priorities.

- Asian-American Donors:
    - Strong support for education, healthcare, and international relief efforts.
    - Giving is often influenced by family traditions and collectivist cultural values.
    - Many Asian-American donors give through religious or community-based organizations.

Age-Related Differences in Giving

Different generations have varying donation behaviors, as noted below:

- Young Adults (18-35):
    - More likely to give to online campaigns, crowdfunding, and peer-to-peer fundraising.
    - Interested in social justice, environmental issues, and humanitarian efforts.
    - Prefer engagement through social media and digital platforms.
    - Value transparency and impact, often choosing organizations with clear reporting on how donations are used.

- Middle-Aged Adults (36-55):
    - Largest donor group in terms of frequency and amount given.
    - Support a mix of causes, including education, health, and local charities.
    - Likely to engage in workplace giving and employer-matching donation programs.

- Older Adults (56+):
    - Give the largest total amounts over time.
    - More inclined to support religious organizations, healthcare, and legacy giving (through wills and estates).
    - Prefer traditional methods like direct mail and planned giving.
    - Tend to remain loyal to specific organizations over long periods.

<u>Income and Giving Patterns</u>

Income level plays a major role in how much people give and to what causes, as noted below:

- Lower-Income Donors:

    o Often give a higher percentage of their income than wealthier individuals.
    o Support local charities, religious organizations, and direct aid efforts (food banks, emergency relief).
    o Likely to engage in informal giving, such as helping family and friends in need.

- Middle-Income Donors:

    o Most common donors to nonprofits and community organizations.
    o Participate in workplace giving and recurring donations.
    o Support education, healthcare, and humanitarian causes.

- High-Income Donors:

    o Donate the largest total amounts, often making major gifts.
    o More likely to contribute through foundations, endowments, and legacy gifts.
    o Prioritize arts, research, higher education, and policy-focused initiatives.
    o Can be influenced by tax deductions and structured giving strategies.

In short, individual donors have diverse characteristics that shape their giving behavior. While altruism is a common motivator, factors such as sex, ethnicity, age, and income influence how, why, and where they donate. Understanding these differences helps nonprofits tailor their fundraising strategies to better engage different donor segments.

The Role of Self-Interest in Donations

While charitable giving is often associated with altruism and social responsibility, self-interest also plays a significant role in why individuals donate to nonprofits. Many donors give not just to help others but also to gain personal benefits—whether psychological, social, financial, or professional. Understanding these self-interested motivations can help nonprofits design more effective fundraising strategies. The key issues are noted below.

Psychological Benefits: Feeling Good About Giving

One of the strongest self-interest motivations for giving is the psychological reward donors receive. For example, many individuals experience a sense of happiness or satisfaction after donating, known as the *warm glow* effect. This positive emotion reinforces continued giving. Or, donors sometimes donate to alleviate feelings of guilt about their own wealth or privileges. Another possibility is that some donors see their giving as a reflection of their personal values, helping them maintain a self-image as ethical and compassionate individuals.

Social and Relational Benefits: Enhancing Reputation & Community Standing

Donating to charities can enhance a person's reputation and social standing. For example, publicized giving (such as naming rights to buildings or donor recognition events) allows individuals to showcase their generosity, thereby boosting their social status. Or, donors may be influenced by their friends, family, or professional circles. If charitable giving is seen as a social norm within a community, individuals may give to maintain their reputation or to fit in. Another possibility is that giving is viewed as a way to build connections with influential individuals, particularly in high-profile charitable events, galas, and business networking circles.

Financial Incentives: Tax Benefits & Strategic Giving

Many donors, especially high-income individuals, take advantage of tax benefits that reduce taxable income when donating to qualified nonprofits. If a nonprofit is not classified by the IRS as a 501(c)(3) – for which donations are deductible – then they will not donate. Or, wealthy donors may structure donations to minimize estate taxes while at the same time creating a philanthropic legacy. Another variation on the concept is when individuals donate because their employers match contributions, effectively doubling their impact while receiving financial benefits.

Political & Business Interests: Influence & Strategic Philanthropy

Some donors contribute to nonprofits aligned with their political beliefs or as a way to indirectly support policy changes. Or, business owners and executives may donate to enhance their company's reputation, attract customers, or align with corporate social responsibility initiatives. A variation on the concept arises when donations are linked to branding and marketing strategies, which help businesses improve their public image while supporting a cause at the same time.

Reciprocity: Giving with the Expectation of Receiving

Some individuals donate with the hope that they will receive future benefits, whether through social connections, professional advancement, or business opportunities. In some cultures and religious traditions, giving is believed to bring spiritual rewards, good karma, or blessings in return. For example, members of the Church of Jesus Christ of Latter-day Saints are expected to tithe 10% of their income, believing that their faithfulness in giving will result in both spiritual and material blessings.

Summary

While charitable giving is often driven by compassion and a desire to help others, self-interest plays a significant role in motivating donors. Whether seeking emotional fulfillment, social recognition, financial benefits, political influence, or business advantages, donors often receive something in return for their generosity. Understanding these self-interested motivations can help nonprofits tailor their fundraising efforts, offering incentives that align with donors' personal goals while advancing their missions.

The Role of Empathy in Donations

Empathy – the ability to understand and share the feelings of others – plays a significant role in motivating individuals to donate to nonprofits. When people feel a strong emotional connection to a cause or the beneficiaries of a charity, they are more likely to contribute time, money, and resources. Empathy influences charitable giving in several key ways, from triggering emotional responses to shaping long-term commitment to causes. The key issues are noted through the remainder of this section.

Emotional Responses: The Power of Feeling Connected

Empathy triggers an emotional reaction when individuals see or hear about the suffering of others. For example, people are more likely to give if they can imagine themselves or loved ones in the same situation as those in need (e.g., parents donating to children's hospitals after experiencing a child's illness). Nonprofits often use storytelling, images, and personal testimonials to evoke empathy and increase donations. For example, disaster relief organizations show images of affected families to encourage giving. Empathy-driven giving is especially common during times of crisis, such as natural disasters, humanitarian crises, or viral crowdfunding campaigns for individuals facing hardship.

The "Identifiable Victim Effect"

People tend to donate more when they can emotionally connect with a single, identifiable individual rather than a large group. This is known as the "identifiable victim effect." Studies show that donors respond more generously when they see a specific face, name, or personal story rather than statistics about large-scale suffering. For example, a nonprofit raising funds for childhood cancer treatment is more successful when featuring one child's story rather than broad statistics about pediatric cancer rates.

Social and Cultural Norms: Collective Empathy

Empathy is often shaped by societal and cultural values, influencing donation behavior in different communities. For example, people are more likely to donate to causes that affect those they identify with, such as veterans supporting military charities or members of religious communities giving to faith-based causes. However, when donors are constantly exposed to overwhelming suffering (e.g., global hunger, war), they may feel emotionally exhausted and so are less likely to give, demonstrating the limits of empathy-driven giving.

Long-Term Commitment & Altruism

While some donations are impulsive, empathy can also drive long-term giving and sustained involvement in charitable causes. For example, donors who feel deep empathy toward a cause often become long-term supporters, committing to monthly giving programs. In addition, empathy does not just lead to financial contributions; it also motivates individuals to volunteer their time and skills.

Conclusion

Empathy is a powerful driver of charitable giving, influencing both spontaneous and long-term donations. By fostering emotional connections, nonprofits can increase donor engagement and support. However, while empathy is a strong motivator, it must be balanced with effective storytelling, social influence, and strategic fundraising efforts to sustain long-term giving.

How Donors Evaluate the Utility of a Donation

When deciding to donate, individuals often assess the utility of their donation, including its impact, effectiveness, and value in achieving the intended goals. Donors want to ensure that their contributions are used efficiently and meaningfully, whether to help people in need, advance a cause, or support a nonprofit's mission. The evaluation process involves both rational and emotional considerations. The main donor considerations are noted below.

Perceived Impact: Will My Donation Make a Difference?

One of the primary ways donors evaluate utility is by assessing the effectiveness of their contribution in creating real-world change. Donors prefer nonprofits that can demonstrate concrete results, such as the number of meals provided, children educated, or medical treatments funded. Some donors evaluate whether their donation contributes to short-term aid (e.g., disaster relief) or long-term solutions (e.g., poverty reduction programs). For example, a donor considering two charities – one that provides emergency food aid and another that funds agricultural training – may weigh whether immediate relief or long-term food security offers greater utility.

Financial Efficiency: How Well Are Funds Managed?

Many donors examine how efficiently a nonprofit allocates and spends donations to determine whether their contribution will be used effectively. Donors often look at financial reports or nonprofit rating agencies (e.g., Charity Navigator, GuideStar, BBB Wise Giving Alliance) to see what percentage of funds go to programs vs. overhead (staff salaries, marketing, administration). Donors may prefer nonprofits that maximize resources with minimal waste, ensuring that donations directly support the mission.

> **Tip:** Organizations that openly share financial statements, impact reports, and independent audits tend to gain more trust.

EXAMPLE

A donor comparing two disaster relief organizations may choose the one that spends 90% of donations on direct aid rather than one that spends 50% on administrative costs.

Personal Values & Emotional Connection

Even though utility is often evaluated rationally, emotional and personal factors strongly influence donation decisions. For example, donors support causes they deeply care about, such as environmental conservation, education, or healthcare. Further, people are more likely to give if they have a personal connection, such as donating to a cancer research foundation after a loved one's diagnosis. This means that (for example) a donor passionate about climate change may prioritize environmental charities over other causes, even if another nonprofit has a higher impact per dollar.

Matching & Leverage: Can My Donation Be Multiplied?

Some donors consider whether their donation can be matched or leveraged for greater impact. For example, many donors prefer giving when their employer or another donor offers to match their contribution, doubling the impact. Other donors choose organizations that can use their donation to unlock additional grants, sponsorships, or government funding. For example, a donor might be more inclined to give during a "Double Your Impact" campaign, where a corporate sponsor matches every dollar donated.

Long-Term Sustainability & Systemic Change

Some donors evaluate the long-term impact of their donation beyond immediate relief efforts. For example, does a nonprofit address root causes (e.g., education programs to reduce poverty) or only treat symptoms (e.g., food aid for the hungry)? Or, will the donation help the community become more independent, or will it create long-term reliance on aid? As another example, donors may prefer nonprofits that use creative, research-backed strategies to solve problems more effectively.

EXAMPLE

A donor may decide to support a nonprofit that provides scholarships and vocational training over one that simply gives direct cash assistance, believing that education leads to long-term financial independence.

Conclusion

Donors evaluate the utility of their donation based on a combination of impact, financial efficiency, personal values, leverage, and long-term sustainability. While some prioritize data-driven effectiveness, others focus on emotional connections or systemic change. Nonprofits that clearly communicate their results, maintain transparency, and offer ways to maximize donor contributions are more likely to attract and retain support.

The Impact of the Social Environment on Donors

While economic factors such as income and tax incentives influence donations, social factors play an equally crucial role in shaping how, when, and why individuals give to nonprofits. The social environment—including social influence, social networks, and social identity—has a significant impact on philanthropic behavior. Understanding these factors helps nonprofits develop strategies to engage donors, foster loyalty, and maximize their fundraising efforts.

We begin by examining social influence, which explains how individuals are swayed by the actions and opinions of others. We then explore the role of social networks, which structure the flow of information and create opportunities for giving. Finally, we analyze social identity and its influence on donor motivation, highlighting how individuals align their giving with their sense of belonging to particular groups.

Social Influence and Charitable Giving

Social influence refers to the ways in which individuals change their thoughts, feelings, or behaviors in response to real or perceived pressure from others. This influence can be direct (e.g., a friend asking someone to donate) or indirect (e.g., observing that others are donating). Social influence plays a key role in charitable giving, as people often look to others when deciding how much to give, where to give, and whether to give at all.

There are several types of social influences that can impact a donor's giving. They are as follows:

- *Normative influence.* Normative influence occurs when individuals conform to social norms—the unwritten rules that govern acceptable behavior in a given community. People donate because they believe it is expected of them or because they want to be viewed positively by others. This is especially evident in public fundraising campaigns where donors' names or contributions are displayed. For example, online fundraising platforms often feature donor lists, which can encourage others to give because they see that their peers are contributing.
- *Informational influence.* Informational influence occurs when individuals look to others for guidance on how to behave, especially in situations where they are uncertain. If a person sees that a trusted friend supports a particular nonprofit, they may be more inclined to believe the cause is legitimate and worthy of support. This type of influence is especially strong when donors

lack direct knowledge about a nonprofit and rely on social cues to make their decision.

- *Peer effects in giving.* Research shows that individuals are more likely to give—and give larger amounts—when they see their peers donating. This effect is amplified in structured settings such as workplace giving campaigns, alumni donation drives, and crowdfunding platforms. In these contexts, donors not only receive direct requests but also see real-time evidence of others' generosity, reinforcing their own willingness to contribute.
- *Social proof.* Social proof refers to the tendency of people to follow the actions of others, assuming that these behaviors are correct. In philanthropy, social proof is evident when donors are influenced by high-profile individuals, celebrity endorsements, or large donor lists. Nonprofits often leverage this by showcasing testimonials, highlighting donor numbers, or publicly recognizing major gifts.

Social Networks and the Spread of Philanthropy

A social network is a structure composed of individuals and groups that are connected by relationships such as friendship, kinship, or shared interests. Social networks facilitate the flow of information and resources, playing a critical role in philanthropy by determining how charitable appeals reach potential donors and how giving behaviors spread.

There are several ways in which social networks play a role in charitable giving, which are as follows:

- *Information dissemination.* Social networks are powerful channels for spreading awareness about causes and nonprofits. Individuals often learn about charitable opportunities through personal relationships, social media, or community groups. When a trusted friend or colleague shares a fundraising campaign, it carries more weight than an impersonal advertisement. Research indicates that donors are more likely to give when they receive appeals from people they know rather than from organizations alone.
- *The strength of weak ties.* The "strength of weak ties" theory suggests that while strong ties (close friends and family) are important for support and influence, weak ties (acquaintances and distant connections) are crucial for spreading new information. In philanthropy, weak ties help introduce individuals to new causes and nonprofits that they might not otherwise encounter. For instance, a person might donate to a disaster relief fund after seeing a distant connection share a compelling story on social media.
- *Social contagion and giving behavior.* Giving behavior spreads through social networks in a phenomenon known as social contagion. When one person donates, it increases the likelihood that their friends, family, and acquaintances will do the same. This effect is particularly pronounced in online fundraising platforms where donation activity is visible. Studies show that when

individuals see a donation notification from a friend, they are significantly more likely to contribute themselves.

- *Network effects in large-scale philanthropy.* At a larger scale, social networks facilitate major fundraising efforts such as viral crowdfunding campaigns. Movements like the ALS Ice Bucket Challenge demonstrate how social networks can rapidly amplify charitable giving. In such cases, individuals not only donate but also encourage others in their network to participate, creating a cascading effect that significantly increases fundraising success.

Social Identity and Philanthropic Motivation

Social identity theory suggests that individuals derive part of their self-concept from membership in social groups. People categorize themselves and others into groups based on characteristics such as nationality, religion, ethnicity, political affiliation, and professional identity. These group memberships influence behavior, including charitable giving. Social identity shapes donor giving in the following ways:

- *In-group favoritism and charitable preferences.* People are more likely to donate to causes that benefit groups with which they identify. This is known as in-group favoritism. For example, alumni often donate to their former universities, members of religious communities support faith-based charities, and individuals with a shared cultural heritage contribute to organizations that serve their ethnic group. Research suggests that in-group favoritism increases both the likelihood and amount of donations.

EXAMPLE

Princeton has one of the highest alumni donation participation rates among Ivy League schools, regularly exceeding 50% of alumni contributing in a given year. A major reason for this is the strong group identity that Princeton cultivates among its graduates. Here are several examples of how this group identity is fostered:

- *Class-based fundraising competitions.* Princeton organizes class-based competitions where different graduating classes compete to see which can achieve the highest percentage of donors. The rivalry between classes (e.g., Class of 1980 vs. Class of 1990) strengthens alumni identity and encourages giving. This competition taps into social pressure and collective pride, leading to increased donations.
- *Ties to prestige and exclusivity.* Princeton alumni see their donations as a way to reinforce their school's elite status. The shared identity as "Princetonians" drives them to support their alma mater financially to maintain its high rankings and exclusivity.
- *Reunion culture and peer influence.* Princeton hosts massive reunions where alumni return to campus in large numbers. At these events, university representatives and peers encourage donations, leveraging nostalgia and group loyalty.

In 2023, Princeton's Annual Giving campaign raised $68.6 million, with 48.9% alumni participation. This level of engagement is far higher than most universities, largely because of the school's ability to foster a strong sense of group identity.

This example shows how a well-established group identity—rooted in competition, exclusivity, and tradition—can drive higher alumni donations at Ivy League universities.

- *Moral and ethical considerations.* Social identity can also shape charitable giving through moral obligations. Members of a group may feel a sense of duty to support causes aligned with their values and collective identity. For instance, environmental activists are more likely to support climate change initiatives, while veterans are more inclined to donate to military charities.
- *Identity signaling through philanthropy.* Individuals use charitable giving as a way to signal their values and identity to others. Public acts of philanthropy, such as sponsoring a charity event or making a high-profile donation, can reinforce a person's social status and credibility within their community. Nonprofits often capitalize on this by offering public recognition, such as naming opportunities for major gifts.
- *Group-based social norms and giving expectations.* Within social groups, giving norms are established that shape donor behavior. In religious communities, tithing or charitable giving may be an expected practice. In professional or alumni networks, there may be an implicit expectation to contribute to fundraising campaigns. These social norms create a sense of obligation that influences donation patterns.

Identity and Competitive Giving

Another interesting effect of social identity is competitive giving, where individuals donate to demonstrate their commitment to a group or cause. This is often seen in fundraising challenges, political donation drives, or rival university alumni campaigns. When donations are publicly visible, individuals may give more to signal their loyalty or compete with others in their social group.

Conclusion

The social environment plays a vital role in shaping charitable giving. Social influence drives donor behavior through norms, peer effects, and social proof. Social networks facilitate the spread of information and philanthropic trends, amplifying charitable engagement. Social identity affects giving preferences, as individuals align their donations with their group affiliations, values, and social norms. By understanding these social dynamics, nonprofits can develop effective fundraising strategies that leverage social connections, reinforce identity-based giving, and create environments where generosity thrives.

EXAMPLE

Following Hurricane Katrina in 2005, there was an overwhelming outpouring of donations to nonprofits like the Red Cross, largely due to the following:

- *Media coverage and public awareness.* News outlets and social media were flooded with images and stories of the devastation, prompting an emotional response from the public. Seeing others donate and share fundraising campaigns created social pressure to contribute.
- *Celebrity and influencer endorsements.* High-profile figures like Oprah Winfrey and George Clooney publicly donated and encouraged others to give. This kind of social influence increases donor participation, as people often model their behavior after public figures.
- *Peer influence and social norms.* Many companies, schools, and communities organized fundraising efforts, making giving a collective social expectation. Employees saw their colleagues donating, and students participated in school-wide charity drives, reinforcing the idea that giving was the "right thing to do."
- *Matching gift campaigns.* Corporations such as Walmart and Exxon pledged to match public donations, creating an environment where individuals felt their contributions would have an even greater impact, further motivating them to give.

This example shows how a combination of media exposure, peer behavior, celebrity influence, and corporate engagement within the social environment can significantly shape donor behavior, leading to increased nonprofit funding.

Summary

This chapter examined the characteristics of individual donors and how demographic factors such as sex, ethnicity, age, and income influence charitable giving. Women were found to donate more frequently but in smaller amounts, while men tended to contribute larger sums to fewer causes. Cultural and racial backgrounds also played a role, with different groups prioritizing faith-based, social justice, or education-related donations. Age and income levels further shaped donation behavior, with younger donors favoring digital giving and older, wealthier individuals supporting legacy and endowment funds. Understanding these patterns enables nonprofits to tailor their fundraising strategies to engage diverse donor segments more effectively.

Chapter 4
Fundraising Planning

Introduction

Fundraising is a critical component of nonprofit sustainability, requiring strategic planning to ensure financial stability and mission fulfillment. A well-designed fundraising framework provides a structured approach to setting goals, analyzing donors, selecting appropriate fundraising methods, and managing resources efficiently. This chapter outlines the essential steps for developing a comprehensive fundraising plan, from goal-setting and budgeting to donor engagement and evaluation. By implementing a data-driven fundraising strategy, nonprofits can maximize their impact and build long-term financial resilience.

The Planning Framework for Fundraising

Effective fundraising is essential for nonprofit organizations to achieve their missions and sustain their operations. A well-structured fundraising strategy provides a roadmap for resource development, aligning financial goals with organizational priorities. This section outlines a comprehensive planning framework that nonprofits can use to develop and implement a successful fundraising strategy. The framework includes key components such as goal setting, donor analysis, fundraising methods, budget considerations, marketing and communication, implementation, and evaluation. The key steps in the planning framework are noted below.

1. Define Fundraising Goals and Objectives

The first step in developing a fundraising strategy is to establish clear, realistic, and measurable goals. These goals should align with the nonprofit's mission and strategic plan, ensuring that fundraising efforts directly support programmatic and operational needs. Objectives should be SMART (Specific, Measurable, Achievable, Relevant, and Time-bound), allowing the organization to track progress effectively. For example, a nonprofit may aim to raise $500,000 within a year to fund a new community outreach program. Goals should also consider short-term and long-term funding needs, ensuring sustainability beyond immediate financial targets. We deal with fundraising objectives again later in this chapter.

2. Conduct a Fundraising Assessment

Before selecting fundraising methods, conduct an internal and external assessment. Internally, this involves reviewing past fundraising performance, analyzing donor retention rates, and evaluating the effectiveness of previous campaigns. Externally, organizations should assess the broader fundraising landscape, including donor trends, economic conditions, and potential competition for funding. This assessment helps identify strengths, weaknesses, opportunities, and threats (SWOT) related to fundraising, allowing for informed decision-making. We cover this topic in more detail in the next section.

3. Identify and Understand the Target Audience

Successful fundraising depends on a deep understanding of a nonprofit's donor base. Organizations should segment their donors based on characteristics such as giving history, demographics, and motivations. Common donor categories include individual donors, corporate sponsors, foundations, and government grant providers. Nonprofits should also distinguish between one-time donors, recurring donors, and major gift contributors. Developing donor personas—fictional representations of ideal donors— can help tailor messaging and outreach strategies to different audience segments.

4. Select Fundraising Methods and Revenue Streams

Nonprofits use a variety of fundraising methods to diversify revenue and reduce financial risk. These methods include the following:

- *Individual giving.* Soliciting contributions from individual donors through direct mail, online giving, and peer-to-peer fundraising.
- *Major gifts.* Securing large contributions from high-net-worth individuals who have a strong connection to the nonprofit's mission.
- *Corporate partnerships.* Engaging businesses in sponsorships, matching gift programs, and cause-related marketing.
- *Grants and foundations.* Applying for funding from private and public grant-making institutions.
- *Events and galas.* Hosting fundraising events such as charity auctions, benefit concerts, and walks/runs.
- *Planned giving.* Encouraging donors to leave legacy gifts through wills, trusts, and estate plans.
- *Earned income strategies.* Generating revenue through social enterprises, membership fees, or merchandise sales.

A successful fundraising strategy often incorporates multiple methods, balancing short-term revenue generation with long-term sustainability.

5. Budget and Resource Allocation

Fundraising requires financial investment and careful budgeting. Nonprofits should allocate resources effectively by estimating the costs associated with various fundraising activities, such as marketing, staff salaries, event planning, and donor stewardship. A cost-benefit analysis can help determine which fundraising initiatives yield the highest return on investment. Additionally, organizations should set aside funds for donor recognition and engagement activities to foster long-term relationships.

6. Develop a Fundraising Communications Plan

Effective communication is crucial in engaging donors and inspiring support. A well-structured fundraising communications plan includes the following:

- *Key messages*. Clear and compelling narratives that convey the nonprofit's impact and urgency of support.
- *Storytelling*. Using real-life success stories to create emotional connections with donors.
- *Marketing channels*. Leveraging digital platforms (social media, email campaigns, websites) alongside traditional methods (direct mail, phone calls, in-person meetings).
- *Call to action*. Encouraging donors to take specific steps, such as making a donation, attending an event, or sharing the campaign with their networks.

Consistency in messaging across all platforms helps reinforce the nonprofit's brand and mission.

7. Implement the Fundraising Plan

Execution is key to a successful fundraising strategy. Organizations should develop a detailed action plan outlining specific tasks, responsibilities, and timelines. A dedicated fundraising team, including staff, board members, and volunteers, should be assigned roles to ensure accountability. Using a donor management system can streamline operations, track donations, and analyze donor behaviors. Regular check-ins and progress reports help keep fundraising efforts on track.

8. Stewardship and Donor Relations

Building strong relationships with donors is essential for long-term sustainability. Stewardship involves acknowledging contributions, demonstrating impact, and maintaining engagement. Best practices include:

- *Prompt thank-you notices*. Sending personalized thank-you messages within 48 hours of receiving a donation.
- *Impact reporting*. Providing donors with updates on how their contributions are making a difference.
- *Exclusive engagement opportunities*. Inviting major donors to special events or behind-the-scenes experiences.
- *Personalized outreach*. Customizing communication based on donor preferences and past giving history.

By fostering donor loyalty, nonprofits can increase retention rates and encourage repeat giving.

9. Monitor and Evaluate Fundraising Performance

Regular evaluation ensures that fundraising efforts remain effective and aligned with organizational goals. Nonprofits should track key performance indicators, such as:

- *Total funds raised.* Measuring overall revenue generated.
- *Donor retention rate.* Assessing the percentage of donors who give repeatedly.
- *Cost per dollar raised.* Analyzing efficiency by comparing fundraising expenses to income.
- *Return on investment.* Evaluating the profitability of different fundraising methods.

Organizations should use data analytics to identify trends, refine strategies, and make data-driven decisions. Fundraising reports should be shared with stakeholders, including board members and donors, to maintain transparency and accountability.

10. Adjust and Refine the Strategy

A fundraising strategy is not static; it should evolve based on performance outcomes, donor feedback, and external conditions. Nonprofits should conduct periodic reviews and adapt their approach accordingly. If a particular fundraising method underperforms, the organization should explore alternative tactics or refine its messaging. Flexibility and innovation are key to sustaining long-term fundraising success.

Conclusion

Developing a comprehensive fundraising strategy is essential for nonprofit organizations to secure the resources they need to fulfill their missions. By setting clear goals, understanding their donor base, diversifying fundraising methods, and implementing effective communication and stewardship practices, nonprofits can build a sustainable funding model. Regular evaluation and adaptation ensure continuous improvement and long-term success. With a strategic and well-planned approach, nonprofit organizations can maximize their fundraising potential and make a lasting impact in their communities.

The Fundraising Assessment

A fundraising assessment is a crucial process that nonprofit organizations conduct as part of their overall fundraising planning. It provides an in-depth analysis of an organization's past and present fundraising efforts, identifies strengths and weaknesses, and offers data-driven recommendations to improve future fundraising strategies. A well-executed assessment ensures that the organization's fundraising goals align with its mission, capacity, and financial needs while optimizing the use of resources. By conducting a thorough evaluation, nonprofits can make informed decisions that enhance donor engagement, increase revenue, and ensure long-term sustainability.

Understanding the Purpose of a Fundraising Assessment

The primary purpose of a fundraising assessment is to evaluate the effectiveness of a nonprofit's existing fundraising efforts and determine the feasibility of its future fundraising goals. This assessment helps organizations understand how well they are engaging with donors, where their funding is coming from, and which strategies are yielding the highest returns. Additionally, it allows nonprofits to identify areas for improvement, such as diversifying revenue streams, improving donor retention, or strengthening grant-writing capabilities.

A fundraising assessment also plays a key role in risk management. Nonprofits that rely too heavily on a single source of funding, such as government grants or major donors, may face financial instability if those sources diminish. By evaluating fundraising efforts, organizations can identify risks and create strategies to mitigate them. Furthermore, the assessment process fosters transparency and accountability, demonstrating to stakeholders that the organization is managing its financial resources effectively.

Key Components of a Fundraising Assessment

A comprehensive fundraising assessment consists of multiple components that analyze different aspects of an organization's fundraising activities. These components include an evaluation of past performance, donor and revenue analysis, fundraising strategy review, organizational capacity assessment, benchmarking, and external factors that influence fundraising success.

Evaluation of Past Fundraising Performance

A nonprofit's past fundraising performance provides valuable insights into trends, successes, and challenges. Organizations should collect and analyze data from previous fundraising campaigns, events, and initiatives to determine their effectiveness. This includes reviewing financial records, campaign reports, and donor engagement statistics to assess return on investment.

Key performance indicators such as total funds raised, donor retention rates, average gift size, and cost per dollar raised help measure fundraising effectiveness. Organizations should identify which fundraising activities generated the highest returns and which underperformed. Additionally, nonprofits should evaluate their fundraising efficiency by examining how much was spent on fundraising efforts compared to the revenue generated.

Donor and Revenue Analysis

Understanding donor behavior is essential for improving fundraising strategies. A donor and revenue analysis examines who is giving to the organization, how frequently they donate, and what motivates their contributions. This analysis involves segmenting donors into categories such as major donors, recurring donors, corporate sponsors, foundations, and one-time givers.

Nonprofits should assess donor retention and acquisition rates to determine how well they are maintaining relationships with existing donors and attracting new ones. High donor attrition rates may indicate issues with engagement, stewardship, or communication. Conversely, strong retention rates suggest that the organization has effective donor cultivation strategies in place.

Another critical aspect of revenue analysis is examining the diversity of funding sources. Organizations that rely too heavily on a small number of donors or a single type of revenue stream may be at risk. Diversifying fundraising efforts by incorporating individual giving, grants, corporate sponsorships, events, and online fundraising can create a more stable financial foundation.

Review of Fundraising Strategies

Nonprofits utilize various fundraising strategies, including annual campaigns, major gifts programs, capital campaigns, planned giving, peer-to-peer fundraising, and online crowdfunding. A fundraising assessment should evaluate the effectiveness of each strategy, determining which methods align best with the organization's mission and donor base.

For instance, if an organization's major gifts program is underperforming, it may need to enhance donor cultivation efforts or improve relationship-building tactics with high-net-worth individuals. Similarly, if online fundraising campaigns are not meeting expectations, the organization might need to optimize its digital presence, refine its messaging, or invest in better technology.

A review of past and current fundraising strategies also involves assessing donor communication and stewardship efforts. Organizations should examine how they are engaging donors through email, direct mail, social media, and other channels. Effective storytelling, transparency, and donor recognition programs contribute to stronger donor relationships and increased giving.

Organizational Capacity Assessment

The success of fundraising initiatives depends on the organization's internal capacity, including staff, technology, infrastructure, and governance. A fundraising assessment should evaluate whether the nonprofit has the necessary resources to execute its fundraising plans effectively.

This includes assessing the skills and experience of the fundraising team, identifying gaps in expertise, and determining whether additional training or hiring is needed. The assessment should also examine whether the organization has the right technological tools, such as donor management software, email marketing platforms, and data analytics tools, to support fundraising efforts.

Another critical factor is leadership and board engagement. Nonprofit boards play a significant role in fundraising by providing oversight, networking opportunities, and sometimes even direct financial contributions. A fundraising assessment should evaluate the board's involvement in fundraising activities and identify opportunities to increase their participation.

Benchmarking Against Industry Standards

To gain a clearer perspective on its fundraising performance, a nonprofit should compare its results to industry benchmarks and best practices. Benchmarking involves analyzing data from similar organizations in terms of size, mission, and geographic location to understand how the nonprofit's fundraising efforts measure up.

Industry benchmarks, such as average donor retention rates, fundraising efficiency ratios, and sector-specific fundraising trends, provide context for evaluating an organization's performance. If a nonprofit's donor retention rate is significantly lower than the industry average, it may indicate a need for improved donor engagement strategies.

Additionally, benchmarking allows nonprofits to learn from successful organizations and adopt best practices that have been proven to work. Studying case studies, attending fundraising conferences, and engaging in peer networking can provide valuable insights into innovative fundraising approaches.

External Factors Affecting Fundraising Success

A fundraising assessment should also consider external factors that impact an organization's ability to raise funds. Economic conditions, donor trends, policy changes, and competition from other nonprofits can all influence fundraising outcomes.

For example, economic downturns may reduce individual giving, while changes in tax laws might affect donor incentives. Additionally, shifts in donor preferences, such as an increasing emphasis on impact-driven giving, can require nonprofits to adapt their messaging and engagement strategies.

Nonprofits should also assess the competitive landscape, analyzing how similar organizations are fundraising and identifying opportunities to differentiate themselves. Understanding the external environment allows organizations to anticipate challenges and adjust their fundraising strategies.

Using the Assessment to Inform Fundraising Planning

Once the fundraising assessment is complete, nonprofit leaders should use the findings to develop a strategic fundraising plan. The assessment's insights help set realistic fundraising goals, allocate resources effectively, and prioritize initiatives that offer the highest return on investment.

A well-informed fundraising plan should outline specific strategies for donor acquisition and retention, set clear revenue targets, and define key performance metrics. The plan should also include a timeline for implementation and assign responsibilities to staff members, board members, and volunteers.

Regularly revisiting and updating the fundraising assessment ensures that the organization remains responsive to changes in donor behavior, economic conditions, and internal capacity. By integrating assessment results into fundraising planning, nonprofits can build a more sustainable financial future and advance their mission more effectively.

Conclusion

A fundraising assessment is an essential component of nonprofit fundraising planning, providing a comprehensive evaluation of past performance, donor engagement, fundraising strategies, and organizational capacity. By analyzing key data points, benchmarking against industry standards, and considering external factors, nonprofits can gain valuable insights into their fundraising effectiveness. The findings from the assessment guide strategic decision-making, helping organizations optimize their fundraising efforts and ensure financial sustainability. A well-conducted fundraising assessment ultimately strengthens donor relationships, enhances revenue generation, and positions the nonprofit for long-term success.

EXAMPLE

Hope Community Shelter (HCS) is a mid-sized nonprofit organization dedicated to providing emergency housing, job training, and social services to individuals experiencing homelessness. Over the years, HCS has relied on a mix of individual donations, grants, corporate sponsorships, and fundraising events to support its operations. However, in recent years, the organization has faced declining donor retention rates and increasing competition for grant funding. To ensure financial sustainability and improve fundraising outcomes, HCS conducted a comprehensive fundraising assessment as part of its strategic planning process. This assessment includes the following steps:

Step 1: Evaluation of Past Fundraising Performance

The first step in the assessment involved a review of HCS's fundraising history over the past five years. Financial records, donor databases, and campaign reports were analyzed to determine trends in revenue generation and donor engagement. Key performance indicators (KPIs) included:

- *Total funds raised annually*. HCS's revenue had stagnated at around $1.2 million per year, despite increasing program expenses.
- *Donor retention rate*. The organization retained only 45% of its donors year-over-year, significantly lower than the nonprofit sector average of 55–60%.
- *Major gifts program*. Contributions from high-net-worth donors made up just 15% of total revenue, indicating underdevelopment in this area.
- *Cost per dollar raised*. Fundraising expenses were high for certain initiatives, such as the annual gala, which had a 40% expense-to-revenue ratio—far above the recommended 20–30%.

These findings suggested that while HCS had a broad base of support, it struggled with donor retention and inefficient fundraising activities.

Step 2: Donor and Revenue Analysis

Next, HCS segmented its donors to understand their giving patterns and motivations. Key findings included:

- **Donor composition**:
  - *Individual donors.* 60% of total revenue (mostly small, one-time gifts).
  - *Corporate sponsorships.* 10%, but declining in recent years.
  - *Foundations and grants.* 25%, with high dependency on a few key funders.
  - *Events and peer-to-peer fundraising.* 5%, largely from the annual gala and 5K run.

- **Recurring giving**: Only 20% of individual donors were enrolled in HCS's monthly giving program, representing an opportunity for growth.
- **Lapsed donors**: More than 30% of donors who gave in the previous two years had not donated again, signaling weak stewardship efforts.
- **Major gifts**: HCS had not fully cultivated relationships with potential major donors, relying instead on event-based solicitations.

The analysis revealed an overreliance on small, one-time donations and limited efforts to secure long-term donor commitments. Additionally, the heavy dependence on grants posed a financial risk if any funders withdrew support.

Step 3: Review of Fundraising Strategies

HCS assessed its current fundraising strategies to identify strengths and weaknesses:

- **Annual giving campaigns**: While successful in acquiring new donors, these campaigns lacked follow-up efforts to retain them.
- **Grant funding**: While HCS had strong grant-writing capabilities, its heavy dependence on a few funders created financial instability.
- **Major gifts program**: There was no formal major donor cultivation strategy, missing opportunities for larger contributions.
- **Fundraising events**: The annual gala was resource-intensive and had a low return on investment. The organization considered scaling it down or replacing it with a more cost-effective initiative.
- **Digital fundraising**: HCS had an outdated website and limited social media presence, hindering online fundraising potential.

Based on these findings, the organization identified three key areas for improvement: enhancing donor retention, expanding major gifts fundraising, and optimizing digital giving strategies.

Step 4: Organizational Capacity Assessment

HCS conducted an internal review of its fundraising capacity, evaluating staff, technology, and board involvement:

- **Fundraising team**: HCS had only two full-time development staff members, limiting their ability to manage major donor relationships and donor stewardship effectively.
- **Technology**: The donor database was outdated, making it difficult to track donor engagement and personalize outreach.

- **Board engagement**: Only 30% of the board members participated in fundraising activities, highlighting an opportunity for greater involvement.

To address these challenges, HCS recommended investing in donor management software, training staff in major gift cultivation, and increasing board member participation in fundraising.

Step 5: Benchmarking Against Industry Standards

HCS compared its fundraising metrics to those of similar organizations. Its findings included the following:

- **Industry average donor retention rate**: 55–60% (HCS: 45%) → indicating a need for better stewardship.
- **Major gifts as a percentage of revenue**: 30–40% (HCS: 15%) → showing a significant opportunity for growth.
- **Expense-to-revenue ratio for events**: Best practice is 20–30% (HCS: 40%) → suggesting event restructuring or elimination.

These benchmarks reinforced the need to focus on donor retention, major gifts, and cost-effective fundraising initiatives.

Step 6: External Factors Analysis

The assessment also considered external influences on fundraising success, which were as follows:

- **Economic conditions**: Inflation and economic uncertainty had reduced disposable income for some donors, requiring more targeted engagement efforts.
- **Giving trends**: Online giving and peer-to-peer fundraising were on the rise, yet HCS had not fully leveraged these channels.
- **Competition**: More local nonprofits were competing for grant funding, emphasizing the need for revenue diversification.

Step 7: Recommendations and Fundraising Plan

Based on the fundraising assessment, HCS developed a strategic plan with the following recommendations:

1. **Strengthen Donor Retention Efforts**
   - Implement a structured stewardship program, including personalized thank-you messages, impact reports, and donor appreciation events.
   - Expand the recurring giving program by promoting monthly donations as a convenient and impactful way to support HCS.

2. **Develop a Major Gifts Strategy**
   - Identify and cultivate relationships with high-net-worth individuals in the community.
   - Train board members and senior staff in major donor solicitation.
   - Launch a "Leadership Giving Society" to recognize major donors and encourage higher contributions.

3. **Optimize Digital Fundraising**

   o Redesign the website for improved user experience and mobile optimization.
   o Increase social media engagement and integrate peer-to-peer fundraising campaigns.
   o Invest in donor management software to track donor interactions and personalize outreach.

4. **Restructure Fundraising Events**

   o Reduce reliance on the annual gala and explore lower-cost alternatives, such as virtual fundraising campaigns.
   o Expand community-based fundraising initiatives, including corporate matching gift programs.

5. **Enhance Board Involvement**

   o Set fundraising expectations for board members and provide training on donor engagement.
   o Establish a "Board Fundraising Challenge" to encourage members to raise funds through their networks.

Conclusion

By conducting a thorough fundraising assessment, Hope Community Shelter identified key weaknesses in its fundraising efforts and developed a data-driven plan to improve financial sustainability. The assessment revealed a need to focus on donor retention, major gifts cultivation, and digital fundraising while optimizing fundraising costs. By implementing the recommended strategies, HCS aimed to increase donor engagement, diversify its revenue streams, and strengthen its long-term financial health.

Fundraising Objectives

Effective fundraising requires clear objectives that guide efforts in acquiring, managing, and utilizing funds efficiently. These objectives vary depending on the organization's goals, donor base, and external environment. They encompass aspects such as short-term and long-term financial needs, donor engagement, and strategic expansion. Additionally, nonprofits must consider market segmentation and behavioral segmentation to tailor their fundraising approaches effectively. This section explores the types of fundraising objectives that nonprofits might set, with a focus on strategies, market segmentation, and behavioral segmentation.

Types of Fundraising Objectives

Nonprofit organizations establish fundraising objectives based on their mission, financial requirements, and growth strategies. These objectives generally fall into several key categories, which are as follows:

- *Revenue generation objectives.* The main objective of nonprofit fundraising is revenue generation. Nonprofits set specific financial goals to ensure that they can cover operational expenses, fund projects, and expand their services.

These objectives may be set annually, quarterly, or for specific campaigns. Revenue generation goals are often based on previous financial performance, projected expenses, and external economic conditions.

Organizations may aim to diversify their revenue streams by securing funds from multiple sources, including individual donations, corporate sponsorships, grants, and fundraising events. A balanced revenue mix reduces dependency on a single funding source and enhances financial stability.

- *Donor acquisition and retention objectives.* Attracting and retaining donors is a crucial aspect of nonprofit fundraising. Acquisition objectives focus on increasing the number of new donors through outreach programs, marketing campaigns, and community engagement. Retention objectives, on the other hand, emphasize strengthening relationships with existing donors to ensure long-term support.

  Nonprofits often aim to improve donor retention rates by enhancing engagement strategies, offering personalized communication, and demonstrating the impact of contributions. Retaining donors is generally more cost-effective than acquiring new ones, making it a key priority in sustainable fundraising strategies.

- *Major gift and legacy giving objectives.* Some nonprofits set objectives to secure large donations from high-net-worth individuals or planned gifts through legacy giving programs. Major gifts provide substantial funding that can be used for capital projects, endowments, or significant initiatives.

  Legacy giving, or planned giving, involves donors including nonprofits in their estate plans, wills, or trusts. Setting objectives for these contributions requires building long-term relationships with donors, educating them about giving options, and ensuring their philanthropic interests align with the organization's mission.

- *Event-based fundraising objectives.* Fundraising events serve as both revenue-generating activities and opportunities for donor engagement. Objectives for event-based fundraising may include increasing attendance, raising a specific amount of funds, or enhancing brand awareness.

  Nonprofits may organize events such as charity galas, auctions, fun runs, or community fairs. Successful event-based fundraising requires careful planning, marketing, and post-event follow-up to maintain donor interest and participation in future initiatives.

- *Grant and corporate sponsorship objectives.* Many nonprofits rely on grants and corporate sponsorships to fund programs and projects. Objectives related to grants often include identifying new grant opportunities, improving grant-writing success rates, and maintaining relationships with funding organizations.

  Corporate sponsorship objectives focus on forming partnerships with businesses that share similar values and missions. These partnerships may involve financial contributions, in-kind donations, or employee volunteer programs. Strengthening relationships with corporate sponsors can provide nonprofits with long-term support and increased visibility.

- *Digital fundraising and online engagement objectives*. With the increasing role of technology in philanthropy, nonprofits set objectives for digital fundraising and online engagement. These objectives may include increasing online donations, improving social media engagement, or optimizing the organization's website for donor conversions.

  Online fundraising strategies involve leveraging crowdfunding platforms, email campaigns, and social media appeals. Effective digital engagement requires personalized communication, compelling storytelling, and interactive content to inspire donor participation.

Fundraising Strategies

To achieve their objectives, nonprofits implement various fundraising strategies tailored to their target audience and organizational capacity. Here are the main strategy types:

- *Annual fund campaigns*. Annual fund campaigns focus on securing recurring donations from a broad base of supporters. These campaigns emphasize general support rather than specific projects, allowing nonprofits to allocate funds where they are most needed. Organizations use direct mail, email, and social media appeals to solicit contributions.
- *Capital campaigns*. Capital campaigns are targeted fundraising efforts that are aimed at raising significant amounts of money for specific projects, such as constructing a new facility or purchasing equipment. These campaigns often have a defined timeline and involve major donors, corporate sponsors, and grant funding.
- *Peer-to-peer fundraising*. Peer-to-peer fundraising involves supporters raising money on behalf of a nonprofit by reaching out to their personal networks. This strategy leverages social connections and digital platforms to increase visibility and attract new donors.
- *Membership programs*. Some nonprofits establish membership programs where supporters contribute a set amount regularly in exchange for benefits such as exclusive content, event access, or recognition. Membership programs help build a loyal donor community and provide a steady revenue stream.
- *Corporate and foundation partnerships*. Partnering with corporations and foundations allows nonprofits to access additional funding sources. These partnerships may involve sponsorships, employee matching gift programs, or cause-related marketing initiatives.

Market Segmentation in Fundraising

Market segmentation is a crucial component of successful fundraising, as it allows nonprofits to tailor their approaches to different donor groups. Market segmentation involves dividing potential donors into distinct categories based on demographic, geographic, psychographic, and behavioral characteristics. More specifically:

- *Demographic segmentation.* Demographic segmentation classifies donors based on factors such as age, gender, income level, education, and occupation. For example, younger donors may prefer digital donation platforms, while older donors may respond better to direct mail appeals. Understanding demographic trends helps nonprofits create targeted messaging and engagement strategies.
- *Geographic segmentation.* Geographic segmentation focuses on donors' locations, which can influence giving behavior. Nonprofits may target local, national, or international donors depending on their mission and fundraising goals. Regional fundraising strategies may include community events, localized marketing campaigns, and outreach initiatives tailored to specific cultural or economic conditions.
- *Psychographic segmentation.* Psychographic segmentation categorizes donors based on their values, interests, and motivations. Some donors are driven by a passion for social justice, while others may prioritize environmental sustainability or medical research. Understanding donor motivations allows nonprofits to craft compelling narratives and appeals that resonate with different audience segments.

Behavioral Segmentation in Fundraising

Behavioral segmentation focuses on donors' giving patterns, engagement levels, and responsiveness to fundraising efforts. This approach enables nonprofits to personalize communication and strengthen donor relationships. Here are several behavioral segmentations to consider:

- *New donors vs. repeat donors.* New donors require different engagement strategies than repeat donors. Nonprofits may focus on education and introductory messaging for first-time donors, while repeat donors may receive personalized updates, loyalty incentives, or invitations to exclusive events.
- *Major donors vs. small donors.* Major donors contribute substantial amounts and often require a high level of relationship management, including personalized interactions and recognition. Small donors, while giving in lower amounts, form the backbone of many fundraising efforts through collective support. Nonprofits develop tiered engagement strategies to cater to both groups effectively.
- *Seasonal and event-based donors.* Some donors contribute only during specific times of the year, such as holiday giving campaigns or annual fundraising events. Understanding these seasonal patterns allows nonprofits to optimize the timing of their appeals and maximize contributions.
- *Lapsed donors.* Lapsed donors are individuals who have previously contributed but have stopped giving. Re-engaging these donors involves targeted outreach, reminders of past impact, and incentives to encourage renewed support.

Conclusion

Nonprofit organizations must set clear fundraising objectives that encompass revenue generation, donor acquisition and retention, major gift programs, event-based fundraising, grants, and digital fundraising efforts. Implementing effective fundraising strategies, such as annual fund campaigns, capital campaigns, and peer-to-peer fundraising, allows organizations to reach their goals efficiently.

Market segmentation plays a vital role in tailoring fundraising efforts to specific donor groups based on demographic, geographic, and psychographic characteristics. Additionally, behavioral segmentation helps nonprofits understand donor engagement levels and giving patterns, enabling them to personalize communication and strengthen relationships. By setting well-defined fundraising objectives and leveraging strategic segmentation, nonprofits can optimize their fundraising efforts, increase donor participation, and achieve long-term success in advancing their missions.

EXAMPLE

The American Red Cross regularly conducts targeted fundraising campaigns to re-engage lapsed donors—individuals who previously donated but have not contributed within a certain period of time. The organization uses a combination of direct mail, email, phone outreach, and digital marketing to reconnect with past donors. Its campaigns include the following activities:

- *Personalized direct mail appeals*. The Red Cross sends personalized letters to lapsed donors, reminding them of their past generosity and emphasizing the impact of their contributions. These letters often include a heartfelt message from beneficiaries, success stories, and a call to action encouraging the donor to give again. By addressing donors by name and referencing their last donation, the organization creates a sense of personal connection.
- *Targeted email campaigns*. Using donor data, the Red Cross segments lapsed donors based on their previous giving amounts, frequency, and campaign preferences. They send customized email messages highlighting urgent needs, disaster relief efforts, or recent achievements made possible by past donations. These emails often include compelling images, testimonials, and a simple "Donate Now" button to streamline the giving process.
- *Phone outreach*. To make the re-engagement process more personal, the Red Cross employs volunteers or donor relations staff to call lapsed donors. These calls serve as a thank-you for past support while also informing donors about current programs that need urgent funding. Conversations often include updates on how donations have been used, reinforcing the donor's previous impact and inspiring them to give again.
- *Social media and retargeting ads*. The Red Cross also uses digital marketing strategies to re-engage lapsed donors. If a donor has previously interacted with the Red Cross website or social media pages, they may see retargeted ads encouraging them to renew their support. These ads may feature time-sensitive appeals, such as disaster relief efforts, matching gift opportunities, or limited-time fundraising challenges.
- *Special incentives*. To encourage lapsed donors to give again, the Red Cross occasionally offers matching gift opportunities, where a corporate partner agrees to double any donations made within a specified timeframe. They also use incentives like exclusive donor reports, invitations to special events, or recognition in donor newsletters to re-engage supporters.

Through these targeted efforts, the American Red Cross successfully reactivates thousands of lapsed donors each year. By combining personalized outreach, data-driven marketing, and compelling storytelling, the organization effectively reconnects with past supporters, fostering long-term donor retention and financial sustainability.

Developing a Social Media Strategy

In today's digital world, social media is an essential tool for nonprofits to increase awareness, engage with supporters, and drive donations. A well-crafted social media strategy allows a nonprofit to build meaningful relationships with its audience, share impactful stories, and ultimately convert followers into donors. To achieve this, nonprofits must develop a structured approach that includes a clear content strategy, audience engagement techniques, and fundraising tactics.

Understanding the Target Audience

A successful social media strategy begins with a deep understanding of the nonprofit's target audience. Before crafting content, it is crucial to identify who the followers are and what motivates them to support the organization's mission.

To gain insights into the audience, nonprofits should analyze their existing supporters through social media analytics, donor databases, and email lists. Understanding key demographics such as age, location, and interests helps tailor content to resonate with the audience. Additionally, conducting surveys or engaging with followers through comments and direct messages provides valuable feedback on what type of content they find most compelling.

Once the audience is identified, creating audience personas can be helpful. These personas represent different supporter types, such as long-term donors, potential volunteers, or individuals interested in advocacy. Each persona should include details such as preferred social media platforms, motivations, and content preferences. By understanding these personas, a nonprofit can customize its messaging to better engage each segment of its audience.

EXAMPLE

Feeding America is the largest hunger-relief nonprofit in the United States. When Feeding America sought to refine its social media presence, it began by analyzing who was most engaged with its mission and who it needed to reach to maximize its impact. As a nationwide network of food banks, its primary audience included individuals facing food insecurity, but the organization also had to engage donors, volunteers, and policymakers who could support its work.

To gain a deeper understanding of its audience, Feeding America leveraged a mix of data sources, including social media analytics, website traffic reports, and donor demographics. One of the key insights from this research was that a significant portion of its online audience consisted of middle-aged and older adults, particularly those who had previously donated to hunger relief efforts or were interested in charitable giving. This demographic was most active on Facebook, where they engaged with stories about families struggling with food insecurity and shared posts that featured solutions to the issue.

In contrast, Feeding America found that younger audiences, particularly Millennials and Gen Z, were more engaged on Instagram and Twitter (now X). These followers responded well to visually compelling content, such as infographics illustrating hunger statistics, behind-the-scenes videos of food bank operations, and interactive Q&A sessions with experts. Many younger followers were also passionate about social justice, so they engaged with posts that connected hunger relief to broader issues like poverty, systemic inequality, and government policies affecting food assistance programs.

Beyond social media analytics, Feeding America also conducted audience research through surveys and focus groups. These efforts revealed that many people misunderstood the scale of hunger in America, with some assuming that food insecurity only affected certain regions or demographics. This insight shaped the nonprofit's content strategy, leading it to create educational campaigns that highlighted the widespread nature of hunger and the diverse communities it impacted.

By clearly identifying these different audience segments, Feeding America was able to craft a targeted social media strategy. For older donors and corporate sponsors, it emphasized impact stories and donor appreciation posts on Facebook and LinkedIn. For younger, activism-driven audiences, it created shareable infographics, behind-the-scenes content, and interactive discussions on Instagram and Twitter.

This approach not only strengthened engagement but also helped Feeding America drive tangible results. By tailoring its messaging to different audiences, the nonprofit increased online donations, mobilized more volunteers, and fostered advocacy for policy changes related to hunger relief. Its ability to identify and understand its target audience allowed it to craft a social media strategy that resonated deeply with supporters and maximized its reach and impact.

Choosing the Right Social Media Platforms

Not all social media platforms serve the same purpose, and nonprofits must be strategic in selecting where to focus their efforts. Each platform has unique advantages, and the choice should be based on where the target audience is most active.

Facebook remains a powerful platform for nonprofits, offering tools for fundraising, event promotion, and storytelling. It allows organizations to build community through groups, live events, and direct engagement with supporters. Instagram, with its emphasis on visual content, is ideal for showcasing impact stories through images, short videos, and reels. Twitter, now referred to as X, is effective for advocacy, real-time updates, and engaging with influencers and policymakers. LinkedIn serves as a valuable platform for connecting with corporate sponsors, potential donors, and industry professionals. TikTok, known for its short and engaging videos, helps nonprofits connect with younger audiences and drive viral awareness campaigns. YouTube, as a video-centric platform, allows for in-depth storytelling through longer videos and impact documentaries.

Selecting the right mix of platforms ensures that content reaches the intended audience in the most effective way. However, instead of trying to be everywhere, nonprofits should focus on the platforms that align best with their audience and resources.

Developing a Content Strategy

A strong content strategy is the foundation of a successful social media presence. Nonprofits must create content that is both engaging and mission-driven, ensuring that it educates, inspires, and encourages action. A well-balanced content strategy includes a mix of storytelling, educational content, engagement-driven posts, and clear calls to action.

Storytelling is one of the most effective ways to connect with supporters on an emotional level. Instead of solely presenting statistics or organizational updates, nonprofits should share real-life stories that highlight the impact of their work. Success stories featuring individuals who have benefited from the organization's programs create a human connection that resonates with followers. Additionally, showcasing behind-the-scenes moments, such as volunteers in action or staff working on a project, helps build authenticity and trust.

Educational content is another essential component of a nonprofit's social media strategy. Sharing informative posts about the cause, relevant statistics, and expert insights positions the organization as a thought leader in its field. Infographics, blog summaries, and explainer videos are effective ways to present complex information in an engaging format.

Engagement-driven content encourages interaction between the nonprofit and its followers. Posts that include questions, polls, and interactive challenges invite supporters to participate in the conversation. User-generated content, such as testimonials or photos from volunteers and donors, also fosters a sense of community. By encouraging followers to share their own experiences and tag the nonprofit, organizations can expand their reach and credibility.

Calls to action are crucial for converting followers into donors. Every nonprofit should have a clear and compelling call to action in their content, guiding supporters toward specific actions such as donating, signing up for a newsletter, attending an event, or volunteering. The language used should be direct and urgent, emphasizing the immediate impact of taking action. For example, instead of simply saying "Donate today," a more effective message could be "Your $10 donation provides clean water for a child in need—give now."

Maintaining a Consistent Posting Schedule

Consistency is key to keeping followers engaged and maintaining visibility on social media. A well-planned posting schedule helps ensure that content is delivered at optimal times without overwhelming the audience.

Creating a content calendar allows nonprofits to organize their posts in advance and maintain a steady flow of content. The calendar should outline the frequency of posts on each platform, the type of content to be shared, and key dates such as awareness days, fundraising campaigns, and major events.

The ideal posting frequency varies by platform. While Facebook and Instagram may perform well with three to five posts per week, Twitter (now X) often requires daily updates to stay relevant in fast-moving conversations. LinkedIn, being a more professional platform, benefits from two to three posts per week, while YouTube and TikTok may require a focus on quality over quantity with one to two videos per week.

Using scheduling tools such as Hootsuite, Buffer, or Meta Business Suite helps streamline the posting process. These tools enable nonprofits to plan content in advance, schedule posts for peak engagement times, and analyze performance metrics to optimize future content.

Engaging with the Audience

Building a strong social media presence requires more than just posting content—it involves actively engaging with the audience. Responding to comments, direct messages, and mentions demonstrates that the nonprofit values its supporters and fosters a sense of community.

Hosting live sessions is an effective way to connect with followers in real time. Live Q&A sessions, virtual events, and behind-the-scenes live streams create opportunities for meaningful interactions. Additionally, running interactive campaigns such as social media challenges, contests, and giveaways helps boost engagement and attract new followers.

Partnering with influencers and ambassadors can also enhance engagement. Collaborating with individuals who have a strong following and align with the nonprofit's mission increases credibility and expands the organization's reach. Micro-influencers, who have smaller but highly engaged audiences, are particularly effective for grassroots campaigns.

Turning Followers into Donors

Once a nonprofit has built an engaged audience, the next step is converting followers into donors. To achieve this, nonprofits must make the donation process seamless, create compelling fundraising campaigns, and offer incentives for giving.

A user-friendly donation process is critical for maximizing contributions. Nonprofits should ensure that their donation page is mobile-friendly, easy to navigate, and requires minimal steps. Embedding donation buttons directly into social media profiles and posts reduces friction and makes it easier for supporters to contribute.

Running targeted fundraising campaigns is an effective way to drive donations. Creating themed campaigns around Giving Tuesday, holidays, or specific initiatives helps generate excitement and urgency. Nonprofits can also leverage peer-to-peer fundraising by encouraging supporters to create their own fundraising pages and share them with their networks.

Providing incentives for donors can increase contributions and retention. Recognizing donors through social media shoutouts, exclusive content, or branded merchandise encourages repeat giving. Monthly giving programs that offer perks, such as impact reports or behind-the-scenes updates, create long-term donor relationships.

Conclusion

A well-executed social media strategy empowers nonprofits to amplify their mission, engage supporters, and drive donations. By understanding their audience, crafting compelling content, maintaining a consistent presence, and leveraging engagement techniques, nonprofits can turn social media followers into dedicated donors. With strategic planning and ongoing optimization, social media can become a powerful tool for creating lasting change.

How a Nonprofit Sets its Fundraising Budget

Setting a fundraising budget is a critical process for any nonprofit organization, as it ensures that fundraising efforts are financially sustainable and aligned with the organization's overall mission and goals. A well-structured budget helps in allocating resources effectively, maximizing return on investment, and maintaining transparency with stakeholders. The process of setting a fundraising budget typically involves several key steps, which are as follows:

1. *Assess fundraising goals and financial needs.* Before creating a fundraising budget, a nonprofit must define its financial objectives. This involves determining how much money needs to be raised to support operations, programs, and long-term initiatives. The organization reviews its strategic plan and financial projections to identify revenue gaps and set realistic fundraising targets. For example, if a nonprofit aims to expand its community outreach program, it must estimate the associated costs, including staff salaries, materials, marketing, and operational expenses. The total required funding then informs the overall fundraising goal for the year.

2. *Review past fundraising performance.* A key component of budget planning is analyzing past fundraising efforts. The nonprofit examines previous campaigns, events, and donor contributions to determine what worked well and what areas need improvement. Metrics such as donor acquisition costs, return on investment (ROI), and fundraising efficiency ratios provide valuable insights.

   If a nonprofit has historically raised a certain amount of money annually through a mix of grants, individual donations, and events, it will use that data to project future fundraising potential. Adjustments may be made based on economic conditions, donor trends, and emerging opportunities.

3. *Identify fundraising strategies and costs.* Once fundraising goals are established, the nonprofit outlines the specific fundraising strategies it will implement and estimates their costs. Each strategy requires different levels of investment. For instance, hosting a gala event may require a substantial upfront cost but could yield significant donations, while email campaigns might be more cost-effective with a lower return per donor.

4. *Allocate resources for staff and technology.* Fundraising efforts require dedicated staff and technology resources. The budget must account for fundraising staff compensation, fundraising software, and marketing costs.

5. *Set up a contingency fund.* Fundraising can be unpredictable, due to external factors such as economic downturns, donor fatigue, or unforeseen crises. To mitigate risks, nonprofits typically set aside a contingency fund within their budgets. This reserve helps cover unexpected shortfalls or emergency expenses related to fundraising activities.

6. *Calculate the fundraising cost ratio.* Nonprofits must ensure that their fundraising expenses are proportionate to the amount raised. A common benchmark is the fundraising efficiency ratio, which measures the cost of fundraising as a percentage of total funds raised. For example, if a nonprofit spends $100,000 on fundraising and generates $500,000 in donations, its fundraising efficiency ratio is 20%. Many organizations strive to keep this ratio below 25% to maintain financial efficiency and donor trust.

7. *Secure board approval.* After finalizing the fundraising budget, the nonprofit's leadership team presents it to the board of directors for approval. The board reviews the projected costs, fundraising strategies, and expected outcomes to ensure alignment with the organization's mission.

8. *Monitor performance.* Once approved, the budget is monitored regularly. Nonprofits track fundraising performance against budgeted expectations and make adjustments as needed. If a specific campaign underperforms, resources may be reallocated to more effective strategies.

Setting a fundraising budget is a strategic process that requires careful planning, analysis, and flexibility. By assessing financial needs, reviewing past performance, identifying cost-effective fundraising strategies, and ensuring responsible resource allocation, nonprofits can maximize their fundraising impact while maintaining financial sustainability.

Summary

This chapter outlined a structured framework for nonprofit fundraising, emphasizing goal setting, donor analysis, and the selection of diverse revenue streams. Organizations were encouraged to assess past fundraising performance, segment donors, and implement tailored communication strategies to enhance engagement. Budgeting and resource allocation were highlighted as essential for maximizing return on investment while ensuring financial sustainability. The importance of donor stewardship, ongoing evaluation, and adaptability in fundraising strategies was also emphasized. By following this comprehensive approach, nonprofits can strengthen their fundraising efforts and secure long-term financial stability.

Chapter 5
Developing a Cogent Case for Donations

Introduction

The essential element of fundraising is the development of a cogent case for donations. Without it, and despite the best-organized fundraising campaign on the planet, donors will not contribute funds. They must see a clear reason to provide funds, or else they will either keep the cash or donate it to some other nonprofit that has done a better job of clarifying why they should be the recipient of donations. In this chapter, we cover the factors involved in making a clear case with donors, as well as how storytelling can be used to maximize donor engagement.

The Development of a Cogent Case

For any nonprofit organization, securing donor funding is a crucial part of sustaining and expanding its impact. Convincing donors to contribute requires more than just a heartfelt appeal—it involves strategic storytelling, data-driven justifications, emotional engagement, and trust-building. Below are the key factors involved in effectively stating a case for why donors should provide funding to a nonprofit.

A Clear and Compelling Mission

At the core of any fundraising appeal is the nonprofit's mission. Donors need to understand exactly what the organization stands for and why it exists. A well-defined mission statement should answer fundamental questions, such as:

- What problem does the nonprofit aim to solve?
- Who does it serve?
- How does it create change?

The mission should be communicated in a way that is both aspirational and action-oriented. A vague or overly broad mission can dilute the appeal, while a clear and specific one helps donors quickly grasp the organization's purpose. The stronger and more urgent the mission, the more likely donors are to feel compelled to contribute.

Demonstrating a Critical Need

Donors are more likely to give when they recognize a pressing and unmet need. A nonprofit must provide clear evidence that there is a real and urgent problem requiring immediate attention. This can be achieved by presenting statistics, research, and testimonials that illustrate the scope and severity of the issue.

For example, a nonprofit addressing homelessness should highlight relevant statistics, such as the rising number of unhoused individuals in a specific region, the causes behind this trend, and the consequences of inaction. However, numbers alone are not enough—human stories should accompany the data to bring the issue to life. Personal narratives from those directly impacted by the problem help potential donors connect on an emotional level.

Proving Effectiveness and Impact

Once a nonprofit has established the need, it must demonstrate that its approach effectively addresses the problem. Donors want to know that their contributions will lead to meaningful outcomes. This requires showcasing measurable impact through the following:

- Success stories of individuals or communities that have benefited from the nonprofit's work.
- Data on how many people have been helped and in what specific ways.
- Evidence of long-term change, rather than just temporary fixes.

For instance, an education nonprofit seeking funding for afterschool programs should not only highlight the number of students served, but also provide data on improved literacy rates, graduation rates, or future career success. When donors see clear evidence of success, they gain confidence that their money will be well spent.

Aligning with Donor Interests and Values

Different donors have different motivations for giving. Some may be driven by a deep personal connection to a cause, while others prioritize measurable social return on investment. Understanding what matters to a specific donor or donor group allows a nonprofit to tailor its case accordingly.

For corporate donors, emphasizing alignment with corporate social responsibility goals and brand reputation may be key. For individual donors, highlighting personal stories and emotional connections may be more effective. Foundations and grantmakers often require a more data-driven approach, focusing on sustainability, scalability, and long-term impact.

By researching donor interests and aligning the appeal with their values, a nonprofit increases its chances of securing funding.

Establishing Credibility and Trust

Trust is a major factor in donor decision-making. Before committing funds, donors need to feel confident that the nonprofit is reputable, well-managed, and transparent. Key ways to build trust include:

- Demonstrating financial responsibility by sharing audited financial statements, annual reports, and budget breakdowns.
- Highlighting endorsements, partnerships, or recognitions from reputable institutions.
- Providing clear information about leadership, governance, and accountability practices.

- Showcasing testimonials from previous donors or beneficiaries who can vouch for the organization's effectiveness.

A nonprofit with a history of responsible financial management and program success will find it easier to gain donor trust.

Storytelling to Inspire Emotion

Facts and figures are essential, but emotions drive action. Donors need to feel personally connected to a cause before they are willing to contribute. Storytelling is one of the most powerful ways to achieve this. A compelling story should include the following:

- Introduce a relatable protagonist (such as an individual or community the nonprofit has helped).
- Describe the challenges they faced before receiving support.
- Show how the nonprofit intervened to create change.
- Highlight the positive outcome made possible by donor support.

For example, rather than just stating that a nonprofit provides meals to families in need, telling the story of a single mother who struggled to feed her children before receiving help makes the need feel more immediate and real.

Offering Multiple Ways to Contribute

Not all donors have the same capacity to give, so providing multiple giving options increases the likelihood of securing funding. These options may include:

- One-time donations for those who prefer a straightforward contribution.
- Monthly giving programs for donors who want to provide sustained support.
- Corporate sponsorships for businesses looking to make a larger impact.
- In-kind donations, such as goods or services that support the nonprofit's mission.
- Legacy giving for donors who want to include the nonprofit in their estate planning.

By diversifying donation options, nonprofits make it easier for potential donors to find a giving method that suits their preferences and financial situation.

Demonstrating Sustainability and Long-Term Vision

Many donors want assurance that the nonprofit will be able to sustain its work over the long term. They are more likely to contribute if they see a well-thought-out plan for growth and sustainability. This includes:

- A clear strategic plan outlining future goals and how funds will be used to achieve them.
- Diversified funding sources to prevent over-reliance on a single donor or revenue stream.
- Plans for scaling successful programs to reach more people.

Donors want to know that their investment will have a lasting impact, not just provide a temporary fix.

Providing Recognition and Engagement Opportunities

Acknowledging donors for their contributions and keeping them engaged increases the likelihood of long-term support. This can be done through:

- Personalized thank-you letters, emails, or phone calls.
- Public recognition in newsletters, websites, or events (with the donor's permission).
- Invitations to site visits, special events, or donor appreciation gatherings.
- Regular updates on the impact of their contributions.

When donors feel appreciated and see how their money is making a difference, they are more likely to remain engaged and continue giving.

Urgency and a Clear Call to Action

A strong case for support must include a sense of urgency. If donors believe they can give at any time, they may delay their decision indefinitely. A nonprofit should communicate why immediate action is necessary, whether it's to take advantage of a matching gift opportunity, respond to an urgent crisis, or meet a critical deadline.

A clear call to action should specify:

- The exact amount needed and how it will be used.
- How donors can give (e.g., online donation, mailed check, etc.).
- The impact their donation will have.

For example, rather than saying, "Please donate to support children's education," a more compelling call to action would be: "A $50 donation today provides school supplies for one child for an entire year. Give now to change a child's future."

Conclusion

Securing donor funding requires a well-structured, emotionally engaging, and data-backed case for support. A nonprofit must clearly articulate its mission, demonstrate a critical need, showcase impact, and build trust with donors. By aligning with donor values, offering multiple giving options, and creating a sense of urgency, a nonprofit increases its chances of securing the necessary funding to continue its work.

Ultimately, donors want to feel that their contributions will make a real difference. By crafting a compelling case that speaks to both the heart and the mind, nonprofits can inspire generosity and build lasting relationships with their supporters.

EXAMPLE

One compelling real-world case for support comes from Save the Children, a globally recognized nonprofit dedicated to improving the lives of children through education, health, and emergency relief. In 2006, the organization launched the "Rewrite the Future" campaign, an ambitious global initiative aimed at providing quality education to millions of children affected by conflict.

The Case for Support: "Rewrite the Future"

1. *A clear and compelling mission.* Save the Children framed the campaign around a powerful and urgent mission: *"To provide quality education to 3 million children in conflict-affected areas, ensuring they have the opportunity to learn and build a better future."*

   The organization emphasized that education is a fundamental right and a critical pathway out of poverty, particularly for children living in war zones.

2. *Demonstrating a critical need.* Save the Children presented stark data to illustrate the severity of the issue:

   - At the time, 43 million children living in conflict zones were out of school.
   - Children in war-torn countries were twice as likely to miss out on education compared to their peers in stable regions.
   - A lack of education increased the risk of exploitation, child labor, early marriage, and recruitment into armed groups.

   To humanize the statistics, they shared stories of children like Aisha, a young girl from Sudan whose school had been destroyed by war. Before the intervention of Save the Children, she had no access to education, but with donor support, she was able to attend a safe learning environment.

3. *Proving effectiveness and impact.* Save the Children showcased its expertise in delivering education programs in crisis settings. They presented evidence that:

   - Schools built and supported by Save the Children had improved literacy rates by 40% in some regions.
   - Training local teachers and providing educational materials had led to higher student retention rates.
   - In past projects, they had successfully reached millions of children, ensuring that donor funds were being used effectively.

4. *Aligning with donor interests and values.* Save the Children tailored its appeals to different donor groups:

   - Individual donors were shown the direct impact their contributions could have on one child's education.
   - Corporate partners were invited to support large-scale infrastructure projects, such as rebuilding schools.
   - Institutional donors and foundations were given long-term impact data and sustainability plans.

5. *Establishing credibility and trust.* The campaign highlighted Save the Children's long-standing reputation, citing:

- Its history of success in over 120 countries.
- Endorsements from global education experts and agencies like UNICEF.
- A commitment to financial transparency, with detailed reports on how donor funds were allocated.

6. *Storytelling to inspire emotion.* In addition to statistics, Save the Children used personal stories and images to connect donors emotionally to the cause. They produced videos showing children's joy as they entered new classrooms, learned to read, and expressed hope for their future. One compelling story was of Juma, a 10-year-old boy from the Democratic Republic of Congo, who had never attended school due to ongoing conflict. After receiving educational support, Juma shared: *"Now, I dream of becoming a doctor so I can help others."*

7. *Offering multiple ways to contribute.* Save the Children made it easy for donors to give through:

- One-time donations: $50 to provide a child with books and school supplies.
- Monthly giving: $25 per month to support ongoing education initiatives.
- Corporate sponsorships: Businesses could fund entire school reconstructions.
- Legacy giving: Including Save the Children in wills or estate plans.

8. *Demonstrating sustainability and long-term vision.* Rather than presenting the campaign as a short-term fix, Save the Children outlined a 5-year plan to build 1,000 schools, train 50,000 teachers, and advocate for government policies supporting education in conflict zones.

9. *Providing recognition and engagement opportunities.* Donors received impact updates, newsletters, and invitations to site visits to see the projects firsthand. Corporate partners were publicly recognized on the organization's website and in campaign materials.

10. *Urgency and a clear call to action.* The campaign emphasized why immediate action was necessary, particularly in active war zones where children's education was at risk every day. Their calls to action included: *"Every day a child is out of school, they fall further behind. Your donation today can change a child's future forever."*

Campaign Outcome

The "Rewrite the Future" campaign successfully raised over $400 million and provided access to quality education for more than 10 million children in conflict-affected areas. Save the Children's case for support was effective because it combined data-driven evidence, emotional storytelling, credibility, and clear calls to action. By aligning with donor values and demonstrating tangible impact, they were able to inspire generosity and create lasting change.

Developing a Compelling Narrative

In the world of nonprofit fundraising, storytelling is one of the most powerful tools to inspire action, engage donors, and build lasting relationships. While statistics and data are crucial for establishing credibility, it is the emotional connection created through storytelling that moves people to give. A well-structured story can illustrate the urgency of a cause, highlight the impact of a donor's contribution, and make abstract issues feel personal and immediate.

To maximize donor engagement, nonprofit storytelling should be structured strategically, following a compelling narrative arc that fosters empathy, urgency, and a clear call to action. This section explores how storytelling can be used effectively by nonprofits to convey the need for donor support and provides a framework for structuring these stories in a way that resonates deeply with potential contributors.

Why Storytelling Matters in Nonprofit Fundraising

Humans are wired for stories. Research in neuroscience has shown that narratives activate more areas of the brain than facts alone, creating emotional connections that drive action. When a nonprofit shares a compelling story, it transforms an abstract cause into a personal experience for the donor, making them more likely to feel a sense of responsibility and urgency.

Storytelling matters in nonprofit fundraising because it does the following:

- *Builds an emotional connection.* A well-told story creates empathy, making donors feel personally invested in the cause.
- *Simplifies complex issues.* Many social issues are multifaceted and difficult to understand through data alone. A narrative provides context and clarity.
- *Demonstrates impact.* A story can illustrate exactly how donor contributions make a difference, reinforcing the value of giving.
- *Encourages action.* People are more likely to respond to a story that evokes emotion and presents a clear way to help.

The Essential Elements of a Compelling Nonprofit Story

For storytelling to be effective, it must follow a structured framework that maximizes donor engagement. The most successful nonprofit narratives include these core elements:

- *The protagonist.* Every great story needs a protagonist—a person or group that the audience can connect with emotionally. The protagonist serves as the lens through which the donor experiences the issue. In nonprofit storytelling, the protagonist is often one of the following:

  o A beneficiary whose life has been changed by the organization's work.
  o A community facing hardship or overcoming obstacles.
  o A volunteer or staff member who plays a key role in driving change.

  To make the protagonist relatable, the story should include specific details about their background, struggles, and aspirations. Donors need to see them as real people, not just statistics.

- *The conflict.* Conflict is the driving force of any compelling narrative. It introduces the challenge or obstacle that the protagonist faces, creating a sense of urgency and emotional investment. In nonprofit storytelling, the conflict could be:

    o A family struggling with food insecurity due to economic hardships.
    o A refugee child unable to attend school because of displacement.
    o An environmental crisis threatening a community's access to clean water.

  The conflict should be presented in a way that highlights both the severity of the issue and the stakes involved if action is not taken. However, it is important to avoid portraying beneficiaries as helpless victims. Instead, they should be shown as resilient individuals in need of support to overcome their challenges.

- *The resolution.* After establishing the conflict, the story must present a resolution that demonstrates how the nonprofit's intervention creates real, meaningful change. This is where donors see the power of their support in action. The resolution should highlight the following:

    o The role of the nonprofit in solving the problem: This could be through a specific program, service, or resource provided.
    o The transformation of the protagonist's life: Show how their situation has improved due to donor support.
    o Tangible results: Use before-and-after comparisons, quotes, or data to reinforce the impact.

  A resolution should leave the donor feeling hopeful and inspired, reinforcing the belief that their contribution can bring about real change.

- *The call to action.* No nonprofit story is complete without a clear and urgent call to action. After engaging a donor emotionally, it is crucial to direct them toward the next step—making a donation, signing up as a volunteer, or advocating for the cause. A strong call to action should be:

    o Specific: Clearly state what is needed (e.g., "A $50 donation provides food for a child for a month.").
    o Urgent: Convey why action must be taken immediately (e.g., "Without immediate support, more children will go hungry this winter.").
    o Easy to Act Upon: Provide a direct link, phone number, or instructions to make giving seamless.

By combining these four elements—a relatable protagonist, an urgent conflict, a clear resolution, and a strong call to action—a nonprofit can create a story that moves donors to action.

Structuring the Story for Maximum Donor Engagement

To ensure that storytelling resonates with donors, it should follow a logical narrative structure similar to classic storytelling techniques. The "Hero's Journey" model, commonly used in literature and film, can be adapted to nonprofit storytelling:

1. *The introduction (setting the scene).* The story should begin by introducing the protagonist and their world before the conflict arises. This helps the audience connect with them on a personal level.

    Example: *Maria, a single mother of two in Honduras, wakes up before dawn every day to prepare her children for school. Despite her hard work, she struggles to provide enough food for her family.*

2. *The problem (presenting the challenge).* Once the audience is invested in the protagonist, the conflict should be introduced. This is where the emotional engagement deepens.

    Example: *Due to ongoing drought, crops have failed, and food prices have skyrocketed. Maria's children often go to bed hungry, affecting their health and education.*

3. *The turning point (introducing the nonprofit's work).* At this stage, the nonprofit's intervention is introduced, demonstrating how donors can be part of the solution.

    Example: *When Maria connected with the local food program supported by [Nonprofit Name], she received monthly food supplies and financial literacy training to start a small business.*

4. *The resolution (showcasing transformation).* The resolution illustrates the positive impact of donor support.

    Example: *Today, Maria's children have enough to eat, and her small business is thriving. With continued support, more families like Maria's can build a brighter future.*

5. *The call to action (inspiring immediate action).* The final step is the call to action, reinforcing the urgency of donor support.

    Example: *Thousands of families still face food insecurity. Your donation of $50 today can provide a family with emergency food supplies for a month. Give now to change a life.*

The Role of Multimedia in Storytelling

While written stories are powerful, incorporating visual and audio elements can make storytelling even more compelling. Photos, videos, and social media campaigns can enhance engagement by bringing narratives to life. A well-produced video featuring interviews with beneficiaries, compelling background music, and impactful imagery can evoke deep emotions and drive donations.

Live storytelling events, such as fundraising galas or webinars, also provide opportunities for donors to hear firsthand accounts from beneficiaries, deepening their connection to the cause.

Conclusion

Storytelling is one of the most effective ways for nonprofits to convey the need for donor support. By crafting compelling narratives that feature relatable protagonists, urgent conflicts, transformative resolutions, and clear calls to action, organizations can engage donors on both an emotional and intellectual level.

When structured strategically and supported by multimedia, storytelling becomes more than just a tool—it becomes a bridge that connects donors to a cause, inspires action, and drives lasting change. By harnessing the power of storytelling, nonprofits can not only raise funds but also build a loyal and engaged community of supporters committed to making a difference.

Summary

This chapter explored the essential components of making a compelling case for donor support, emphasizing the importance of a clear mission, demonstrated need, and proven impact. Nonprofits need to align their messaging with donor values, establish trust through transparency, and use storytelling to create emotional connections. Additionally, offering multiple giving options and presenting a strong call to action helps maximize donor engagement. The chapter highlighted how urgency and sustainability play key roles in securing long-term support. Ultimately, a well-crafted case for support combined data-driven evidence with an emotional appeal to inspire generosity among donors and drive meaningful change.

Chapter 6
Types of Fundraising

Introduction

Fundraising success depends not only on a nonprofit's ability to make a strong case for support but also on how effectively it reaches potential donors. Different types of fundraising are needed to ensure that a nonprofit benefits from a balanced and broad-based set of funding sources. This chapter explores the strategies, challenges, and best practices associated with the main types of fundraising, helping organizations maximize their outreach and fundraising impact.

Direct Response Fundraising

Direct response fundraising is a critical strategy for nonprofit organizations seeking to secure financial support from individuals, businesses, and other donors. Unlike general fundraising efforts, direct response fundraising involves soliciting immediate action from potential donors through direct and personalized communication channels. These campaigns are highly measurable and designed to elicit a specific response, such as making a donation, signing up for a newsletter, or attending an event.

This section explores the nature of direct response fundraising for nonprofits, including its key components, strategies, challenges, and best practices for success.

Understanding Direct Response Fundraising

Direct response fundraising is a targeted approach that encourages individuals to take immediate action. It is based on principles of direct marketing, where messages are designed to prompt a direct and trackable response from the recipient. Unlike general awareness campaigns, direct response fundraising focuses on measurable results, such as donation rates, response rates, and return on investment.

Nonprofits use various channels to execute direct response fundraising campaigns, including the following:

- *Billboards*. Billboards can be an effective tool in a nonprofit's fundraising campaign, particularly for raising awareness and driving engagement on a large scale. While billboards are not a direct response medium in the traditional sense, they serve as a powerful way to generate brand recognition, reinforce campaign messaging, and guide potential donors toward taking action through other channels.
- *Direct mail*. Direct mail remains one of the most effective and widely used fundraising tools for nonprofits. Despite the rise of digital communication, direct mail continues to generate strong response rates because it offers a tangible, personalized connection with donors. A well-crafted direct mail

campaign can evoke emotion, build trust, and encourage both new and existing supporters to contribute.

- *Email marketing.* Email marketing is a powerful and cost-effective tool for nonprofit fundraising campaigns, allowing organizations to reach donors quickly and efficiently. Unlike traditional direct mail, email provides an immediate way to communicate with supporters, share compelling stories, and encourage donations with just a few clicks.

Tip: It is essential to build an email list of potential donors, so that you can periodically contact them regarding donations. This can be done in any of the following ways:

- Create a "Join Our List" box on your website (or consider installing a pop-up form)
- Include an email list link on all social media posts.
- Gather addresses in-person and at fundraising events.
- Incorporate email sign-ups into the donation process.

- *Telemarketing.* Telemarketing can be a highly effective tool for nonprofit fundraising campaigns, providing a personal and direct way to connect with donors. Unlike other forms of communication such as email or direct mail, telemarketing allows for real-time conversations, giving nonprofits the opportunity to build relationships, answer questions, and address potential concerns.
- *Digital advertising.* Digital advertising is a powerful tool for nonprofit fundraising campaigns, allowing organizations to reach a broad audience, target specific donor segments, and drive immediate action. Through platforms such as Google Ads, social media advertising, and display networks, nonprofits can promote their campaigns to potential supporters across various digital channels. Digital ads are especially effective for acquiring new donors, retargeting website visitors, and amplifying fundraising efforts during key giving periods.
- *Text messaging.* Text messaging is an effective tool for nonprofit fundraising campaigns, offering a direct and immediate way to engage donors. With high open rates and quick response times, text messages allow organizations to reach supporters instantly and prompt them to take action. Whether used for emergency appeals, recurring donation requests, or donor engagement efforts, text messaging provides a convenient and personal way to connect with donors and drive contributions.

What makes direct response fundraising effective is its focus on immediacy and measurable outcomes, ensuring that nonprofits can adjust their strategies based on real-time data.

> **Tip:** Google Ad Grants is a program by Google that provides free advertising credits to eligible nonprofit organizations. Through this program, nonprofits can receive up to $10,000 per month in free Google Ads to promote their causes on Google Search. These ads appear on Google Search results (not YouTube), and must be text-only. Only registered nonprofits in eligible countries can apply (educational institutions and government entities are not eligible).

Targeting for Direct Response Fundraising

Targeting is a fundamental element in developing a direct response fundraising campaign for a nonprofit, as it allows organizations to reach the right audience with the right message at the right time. By identifying and segmenting potential donors based on various factors such as demographics, giving history, interests, and engagement levels, nonprofits can maximize their fundraising effectiveness and optimize their return on investment. A well-targeted campaign ensures that resources are used efficiently and that donors receive messages that resonate with their values and motivations, increasing the likelihood of a positive response.

The first step in targeting is identifying the ideal donor profile. This involves analyzing past donor data to determine common characteristics among those who have given before. Factors such as age, income level, geographic location, and past donation amounts provide valuable insights. Nonprofits often rely on donor databases and CRM (Customer Relationship Management) software to track and segment this information. By understanding who has historically supported the organization, fundraisers can create targeted outreach strategies that appeal to similar prospects.

Beyond basic demographics, behavioral targeting plays a crucial role in refining the audience. Looking at donors' past interactions with the nonprofit—such as their frequency of giving, preferred donation channels, and responses to previous campaigns—helps shape personalized messaging. For example, a donor who consistently gives online may be more responsive to an email or social media appeal rather than a direct mail solicitation. Similarly, a lapsed donor—someone who has given in the past but not recently—might require a re-engagement campaign with a tailored message reminding them of their past support and the impact they can still make.

Psychographic targeting goes even deeper by considering donors' values, beliefs, and emotional triggers. Nonprofits can gather this data through surveys, social media interactions, and engagement tracking. For example, an environmental nonprofit may have donors who are passionate about conservation, while another segment is particularly motivated by climate change activism. Understanding these differences allows for more customized messaging that aligns with donors' core motivations, making them more likely to contribute.

Once a nonprofit has identified and segmented its target audience, it can create customized messaging and calls to action that align with each group's interests and behaviors. Personalization is key in direct response fundraising, as it fosters a stronger connection between the donor and the cause. Instead of sending a generic appeal, fundraisers can use a donor's name, reference their past giving history, and tailor the message to reflect their known interests. For instance, a donor who previously supported a children's education program may receive an appeal highlighting the impact of their contributions on students' lives, reinforcing the personal connection.

Channel selection is another crucial aspect of targeting in direct response fundraising. Different donor segments prefer different communication channels, and using the right one can significantly improve response rates. Older donors may respond better to direct mail or phone calls, while younger, tech-savvy donors are more likely to engage with email, social media, or text messaging. Multi-channel strategies—where nonprofits reach out through a combination of email, social media, direct mail, and phone calls—can be highly effective in ensuring that messages reach donors in their preferred ways.

Timing is another critical consideration in targeting. Certain times of the year are more conducive to fundraising success, such as the holiday season, Giving Tuesday, or the end of the fiscal year when donors may be looking for tax-deductible giving opportunities. Additionally, donor segmentation can help identify the best timing for specific groups. Recurring donors might benefit from a mid-year impact update that encourages them to continue their support, while first-time donors may respond better to an immediate follow-up reinforcing the importance of their initial gift.

Testing and data analysis further refine targeting strategies. A/B testing—where two versions of a fundraising appeal are sent to different donor groups—allows nonprofits to measure which approach is more effective. By analyzing response rates, donation amounts, and engagement levels, organizations can continuously improve their targeting strategies. Over time, this data-driven approach ensures that fundraising efforts become increasingly effective, leading to higher donor retention and increased contributions.

Retargeting is another powerful technique that enhances direct response fundraising efforts. If a donor visits a nonprofit's website but does not complete a donation, digital retargeting can serve them ads or reminder emails encouraging them to return and contribute. This strategy is especially effective in online fundraising, where many potential donors may show initial interest but need additional prompting to complete their gift.

Ultimately, effective targeting in direct response fundraising is about creating meaningful connections with donors by understanding their preferences, motivations, and behaviors. Nonprofits that invest in data analysis, segmentation, personalized messaging, and strategic channel selection can significantly enhance their fundraising success. By continuously refining their targeting approach based on donor insights and campaign performance, organizations can build stronger donor relationships and drive long-term support for their mission.

> **Tip:** Remarketing is a digital marketing strategy used to re-engage visitors who have previously interacted with a website but left without completing a desired action, such as making a donation. Their interaction can be tracked through digital tools such as Google Ads, Facebook Pixel, or email automation platforms. Once identified, a visitor can be included in a remarketing audience. From there, the nonprofit can deploy targeted marketing efforts to bring them back, such as email campaigns, social media ads, and display ads. In essence, remarketing keeps a nonprofit's mission in front of potential donors and reinforces the reasons why they initially engaged with the site.

Selecting the Best Media for Direct Response Fundraising

Determining the correct form of media for a direct response fundraising campaign for a nonprofit requires a strategic approach that considers the target audience, campaign objectives, budget, and the strengths of each media channel. The right media choice ensures that the message reaches potential donors effectively and maximizes engagement, leading to higher response rates and fundraising success. A well-planned media strategy can make the difference between a highly effective campaign and one that fails to generate meaningful support.

The first step in selecting the appropriate media is understanding the target audience. Different donor segments prefer different forms of communication, and using the right medium can significantly impact engagement. For instance, older donors, who may be more accustomed to traditional forms of communication, often respond better to direct mail and phone calls. In contrast, younger donors, who are more digitally engaged, are more likely to respond to email, social media campaigns, or text message appeals. Conducting donor research through surveys, past campaign data, and donor relationship management tools helps nonprofits identify how different segments prefer to be contacted.

The campaign's objectives also play a crucial role in media selection. If the goal is donor acquisition, digital channels such as social media advertising, email, and search engine marketing can effectively reach new prospects. If the objective is donor retention or increasing gift sizes, personalized direct mail or phone calls may be more appropriate, as they create a stronger emotional connection with existing supporters. For urgent appeals, such as disaster relief or emergency funding needs, email and text messaging provide an immediate way to reach donors and prompt quick action.

Budget considerations are also critical when choosing the right media. Traditional media channels like direct mail and telemarketing can be effective but are often more expensive due to printing, postage, and staffing costs. Digital channels, on the other hand, can be more cost-effective, allowing nonprofits to reach a large audience with a lower investment. However, digital fundraising requires expertise in online marketing, content creation, and data analytics to be successful. Nonprofits should assess their available resources and determine which channels will provide the best return on investment.

The nature of the nonprofit's cause and messaging should also influence media choice. If a campaign relies heavily on storytelling and emotional appeal, video content shared through social media, email, or even television ads can be highly effective.

Videos allow nonprofits to showcase real stories, compelling visuals, and testimonials that resonate deeply with donors. On the other hand, if a campaign is focused on providing detailed impact reports or complex information, direct mail or email newsletters may be a better choice, as they allow for more in-depth communication.

Testing and data analysis are essential in determining the most effective media for a direct response fundraising campaign. A/B testing—where nonprofits test different media formats, subject lines, or messaging variations—helps identify which channels generate the highest engagement and conversion rates. For example, an organization might test an email appeal against a social media ad to see which one results in more donations. Over time, tracking metrics such as open rates, click-through rates, and donation conversions helps refine the media strategy and improve future campaigns.

A multi-channel approach often yields the best results, as donors are exposed to the campaign across different touchpoints, reinforcing the message. For example, a nonprofit may send an initial fundraising email, followed by a direct mail letter and social media ads that remind donors about the campaign. This approach ensures that potential donors receive the message in multiple ways, increasing the likelihood of engagement. However, it is important to maintain consistent messaging and branding across all channels to create a cohesive and compelling donor experience.

Ultimately, choosing the correct form of media for a direct response fundraising campaign requires a balance of donor insights, campaign goals, budget constraints, and media effectiveness. By leveraging data-driven decision-making, testing different channels, and adopting a multi-channel approach, nonprofits can maximize their reach and impact, ensuring that their fundraising efforts resonate with donors and drive meaningful contributions.

Common Challenges in Direct Response Fundraising

While direct response fundraising is effective, it also presents challenges, including the following:

- *Donor fatigue.* Repeated solicitations can lead to donor fatigue, where individuals become overwhelmed or disengaged. To combat this, nonprofits should vary their messaging to avoid repetitive appeals and provide donors with options to choose how often they receive communications.
- *Rising costs.* The cost of direct mail, digital advertising, and telemarketing can add up. To manage costs effectively, nonprofits must test campaigns on a smaller scale before expanding, while also focusing on high-return segments, such as past donors and engaged supporters.
- *Competition for attention.* Nonprofits must compete for donor attention amid numerous charitable appeals. To stand out, they should use visually appealing and emotionally compelling storytelling, while also personalizing messages based on the interests of their donors.
- *Privacy and data protection issues.* With increasing concerns about data privacy, nonprofits must ensure that they follow all applicable data protection regulations, while also ensuring that all donor information is properly encrypted.

Best Practices for Effective Direct Response Fundraising

To maximize the impact of direct response fundraising, nonprofits should adopt the following best practices:

- *Personalization.* Using a donor's name, referencing past contributions, and tailoring messages to their interests can significantly improve response rates. Personalized appeals foster a sense of connection and trust.
- *Strong calls to action.* Every campaign should have a clear and compelling call to action, such as "Join our monthly giving program and make a lasting impact."
- *A/B testing and optimization.* Nonprofits should test different subject lines, messaging styles, and formats to see what resonates best with their audience. A/B testing helps refine strategies for higher engagement.
- *Storytelling with impact.* Rather than simply asking for money, nonprofits should illustrate the tangible effects of donations. Sharing stories of beneficiaries, impact reports, and donor testimonials can enhance credibility and motivation.
- *Invest in technology.* Using donor management software, email automation, and data analytics tools can streamline campaigns and improve efficiency.
- *Conduct follow-ups.* Following up with donors after a contribution strengthens relationships and increases retention. This could include immediate thank-you emails and personalized acknowledgement letters.
- *Diversify fundraising channels.* A diverse fundraising strategy reduces dependency on one channel. Combining digital, print, phone, and in-person appeals ensures broader reach and resilience.

Conclusion

Direct response fundraising is a powerful tool for nonprofits to generate immediate donations and engage supporters. By using targeted appeals, compelling storytelling, and data-driven strategies, organizations can effectively reach donors and inspire action. However, it requires careful planning, consistent optimization, and donor-centric engagement to achieve long-term success.

By addressing challenges such as donor fatigue, rising costs, and competition for attention, nonprofits can refine their approach and build lasting relationships with supporters. When executed effectively, direct response fundraising not only secures vital funds but also fosters a dedicated community of donors committed to the organization's mission.

EXAMPLE

Charity: Water, one of the best-known nonprofit organizations in the world, has successfully leveraged digital public relations to transform the way people engage with philanthropy. Charity: Water focuses on providing clean and safe drinking water to communities in developing countries. Unlike traditional nonprofit fundraising models, Charity: Water has embraced innovative digital strategies to build brand awareness, engage supporters, and inspire action.

Through a combination of social media engagement, influencer partnerships, storytelling, and search engine optimization, Charity: Water has built a global movement, raising over $750 million and funding more than 111,000 water projects worldwide. Their digital PR approach demonstrates how a nonprofit can use online platforms to create transparency, inspire generosity, and establish itself as a leader in its field.

Building a Strong Digital Presence

From the beginning, Charity: Water prioritized a sleek, visually compelling, and user-friendly website. Unlike many traditional nonprofits, which often feature cluttered and outdated sites, Charity: Water designed an immersive digital experience that immediately engages visitors. The website acts as the central hub for all of the organization's public relations efforts, offering clear messaging, impactful storytelling, and an easy-to-navigate donation process.

Their website also incorporates strong search engine optimization strategies, ensuring that people searching for terms like "clean water nonprofit" or "charity donations for water" can easily find them. By consistently publishing high-quality content, such as blog posts, project updates, and success stories, Charity: Water has strengthened its online authority and visibility.

Leveraging Social Media for PR Success

One of Charity: Water's most effective digital PR strategies has been its use of social media to tell compelling stories and engage audiences worldwide. The organization has built a strong presence on platforms like Instagram, Facebook, and LinkedIn, using each platform to connect with different segments of its audience.

Their social media campaigns are centered around powerful visuals and personal narratives. By sharing real-life stories of individuals who have benefited from their water projects, Charity: Water makes its mission tangible and emotionally resonant. High-quality photos and videos showcasing water crises, community impact, and donor contributions allow supporters to see the direct effects of their generosity.

Additionally, the organization strategically uses hashtags to increase visibility and engagement. Campaigns like #NothingIsCrazy and #TheSpring (a monthly giving program) have gained traction, encouraging supporters to participate and share content. By fostering user-generated content—such as supporters posting birthday fundraisers or personal donation stories—Charity: Water has built a highly engaged digital community.

Influencer Partnerships and Celebrity Endorsements

Charity: Water has also utilized influencer marketing as a key part of its digital PR strategy. By partnering with well-known celebrities, social media influencers, and tech entrepreneurs, the nonprofit has expanded its reach to millions of potential donors.

One of the most notable influencer collaborations was with YouTuber Casey Neistat, who created a viral video about Charity: Water that received millions of views. The video not only increased awareness but also inspired a surge of donations from Neistat's audience. Other celebrities, including Will Smith, Kristen Bell, and Tony Hawk have also supported the cause, helping the nonprofit gain credibility and media attention.

Beyond celebrity endorsements, Charity: Water actively engages with micro-influencers—individuals with smaller but highly engaged audiences. These influencers often share their personal fundraising efforts and encourage their followers to contribute, creating a ripple effect of awareness and generosity.

Transparent and Interactive Storytelling

One of Charity: Water's defining PR strategies is its commitment to transparency. Unlike traditional nonprofits that sometimes struggle with donor trust, Charity: Water created a digital-first approach to accountability. Through their "100% Model," the organization guarantees that every dollar donated goes directly to water projects, with separate funding covering operational costs.

To reinforce this transparency, Charity: Water developed an interactive digital map that allows donors to track their contributions in real time. Every funded water project is documented with GPS coordinates, photos, and progress updates, providing tangible proof of impact. This level of openness not only strengthens trust but also encourages repeat donations and word-of-mouth advocacy.

Additionally, Charity: Water has produced documentary-style video content that follows the journey of a donation—from the moment someone gives to the completion of a water project. By humanizing the donation process, the nonprofit makes supporters feel like active participants in solving the water crisis.

Digital Fundraising Campaigns That Go Viral

Charity: Water's digital PR strategy is deeply intertwined with its innovative fundraising campaigns. Instead of relying solely on traditional donation appeals, the organization has created viral digital movements that encourage individual supporters to take action.

One of the most successful campaigns was the "Birthday Campaign," where supporters pledged their birthdays to raise funds for clean water instead of receiving gifts. The campaign gained massive traction when founder Scott Harrison launched it by donating his own birthday, raising thousands of dollars. Over the years, celebrities and everyday supporters alike have joined the movement, leading to millions in donations.

Another notable campaign, "The Spring," was introduced as a subscription-based giving program. The nonprofit used digital storytelling to frame monthly donors as members of an exclusive, impact-driven community. The campaign's success was fueled by social media promotion, email marketing, and influencer advocacy, turning one-time donors into long-term supporters.

Engaging with Online Media and Press

A key part of Charity: Water's digital public relations strategy has been securing media coverage in top-tier digital publications. By strategically pitching their story to outlets like The New York Times, Forbes, and Fast Company, the nonprofit has gained widespread recognition.

Rather than relying on generic press releases, Charity: Water crafts compelling narratives that appeal to journalists. Stories about the organization's innovative approach, technological integrations, and founder Scott Harrison's personal journey have been featured in major news outlets, increasing credibility and visibility.

In addition to traditional news coverage, the nonprofit has embraced podcast interviews, TED Talks, and YouTube collaborations to expand its reach. Scott Harrison's TED Talk, which has amassed millions of views, serves as an evergreen public relations tool that continues to introduce new audiences to Charity: Water's mission.

Harnessing Email Marketing and Digital Outreach

Charity: Water's digital public relations success is also driven by an effective email marketing strategy. Instead of sending generic donation appeals, the organization crafts personalized emails that share impact stories, project updates, and donor spotlights.

By segmenting their email list, they tailor messaging based on donor behavior and engagement levels. First-time donors receive welcome emails with background information about the nonprofit, while recurring supporters receive exclusive content that reinforces their ongoing impact.

Additionally, Charity: Water uses email marketing to encourage peer-to-peer fundraising, providing supporters with digital toolkits and promotional materials to share with their networks. This approach has turned thousands of individual donors into brand ambassadors, further amplifying the nonprofit's reach.

Conclusion

Charity: Water's success is a testament to the power of digital public relations in the nonprofit sector. By embracing a digital-first approach that prioritizes storytelling, transparency, social media engagement, and influencer collaborations, the organization has redefined what it means to fundraise in the digital age.

Major Gift Fundraising

Nonprofit organizations depend heavily on diverse funding sources to sustain their operations and effectively deliver on their missions. Among these varied sources, major donors represent a critical segment whose contributions can significantly influence the nonprofit's ability to expand its reach, amplify impact, and achieve long-term sustainability. Pursuing major donors strategically and effectively is crucial for several reasons.

First, the magnitude of financial contributions from major donors often surpasses what can be raised through smaller, individual donations or traditional fundraising events. Major gifts, typically defined as substantial contributions from individuals, foundations, or corporate entities, can offer nonprofits transformative financial support that substantially advances organizational goals. Such large-scale funding can support ambitious projects, enable facility expansions, and drive innovative programs that would otherwise remain unfeasible due to financial constraints.

Second, securing major donors helps nonprofits achieve a level of financial stability that smaller, intermittent donations cannot provide. Major gifts often create a foundation of predictable funding, allowing nonprofit leaders to plan strategically for long-term initiatives rather than focusing primarily on short-term budget gaps. This predictability permits nonprofits to allocate resources more effectively, strengthen operational capacity, and ensure continuity in vital programs that directly benefit communities served.

Furthermore, relationships with major donors extend beyond financial contributions; these individuals and entities frequently offer nonprofits access to invaluable networks, expertise, and resources. Major donors are often influential figures with considerable connections across sectors. Their association with the nonprofit can bolster the organization's visibility and credibility, opening doors to new partnerships, media opportunities, and additional funding streams. This ripple effect enhances the nonprofit's capacity to advocate for its mission and expand its stakeholder base.

Another significant reason for pursuing major donors lies in the potential for enhanced organizational resilience during economic fluctuations. Nonprofits reliant solely on smaller contributions and public grants may experience severe instability during economic downturns. Conversely, major donors often have greater financial stability and remain capable of providing meaningful support even during challenging financial climates. Consequently, a well-developed major donor strategy serves as a protective mechanism, safeguarding the nonprofit against unforeseen fiscal difficulties and enabling continued impact during turbulent periods.

In addition, cultivating strong relationships with major donors aligns closely with long-term stewardship goals. Nonprofits thrive on building sustained relationships, fostering donor loyalty, and ensuring long-term involvement. Engaging deeply and authentically with major donors strengthens their connection to the mission, motivating continued generosity and deeper levels of commitment. This ongoing relationship encourages donors to transition from one-time benefactors to dedicated partners and advocates, substantially amplifying their lifetime value to the organization.

Finally, actively pursuing major donors contributes significantly to organizational credibility and reputation. A robust roster of notable and respected supporters lends legitimacy to a nonprofit's work and encourages broader community trust and investment. Potential supporters are more inclined to contribute when recognizing that influential community leaders and philanthropists endorse the organization's impact and direction.

In conclusion, actively pursuing major donors is integral to nonprofit sustainability and effectiveness. Major donor relationships provide transformative funding, enhance financial predictability, offer invaluable networking opportunities, build resilience during economic uncertainty, foster meaningful long-term stewardship, and boost organizational credibility. Nonprofits that prioritize and invest strategically in cultivating these pivotal relationships significantly strengthen their capacity to fulfill and expand their essential missions.

Characteristics of Major Donors

Major donors constitute an essential component of nonprofit fundraising strategies, and understanding their characteristics is pivotal for organizations seeking to build effective, long-lasting relationships. While major donors differ widely in terms of their backgrounds, motivations, and giving capacities, they share several common traits and characteristics that can inform targeted engagement strategies.

One of the defining characteristics of major donors is their significant financial capacity. Major donors typically have substantial disposable income or assets, allowing them to make considerable philanthropic contributions. They may have earned wealth through business enterprises, investments, inheritances, or professional careers. Their financial security empowers them to support causes that align closely with their values, ambitions, or personal interests at levels far beyond the typical individual donor.

Beyond financial means, major donors generally exhibit deep passion and commitment toward specific causes or societal issues. They often seek to support nonprofit organizations whose missions align closely with their personal values, convictions, and experiences. Frequently, a personal connection or experience motivates their generosity—such as overcoming illness, responding to community needs, honoring loved ones, or supporting educational or cultural advancement. This emotional or personal resonance can profoundly influence their giving decisions, prompting substantial and sustained philanthropic investments.

Another notable characteristic of major donors is their desire for meaningful engagement and involvement with the organizations they support. Unlike smaller donors who might prefer minimal interaction, major donors typically expect—and appreciate—a personalized relationship. They often desire transparency, direct access to organizational leaders, detailed updates on the impact of their contributions, and opportunities for involvement beyond financial giving. This engagement could include participation in events, volunteering time and expertise, or providing strategic advice and leadership. Their involvement strengthens their sense of personal connection and ownership in the nonprofit's success and fosters lasting partnerships built on trust and mutual respect.

Additionally, major donors frequently display an interest in strategic, measurable impact. They prefer clear visibility into how their gifts advance the organization's mission and create tangible, demonstrable outcomes. Therefore, nonprofits must clearly articulate the intended use of contributions, reporting measurable results that validate the donor's decision to invest generously. In practice, this often means major donors seek comprehensive, outcome-focused reporting, data-driven evaluations, and testimonials showcasing the transformative effects of their philanthropy.

Moreover, major donors often exhibit leadership characteristics and influence within their social or professional communities. They may hold prominent roles in business, government, or society, granting them significant public recognition, networks, and reputations. Such influence can be a critical asset for nonprofits, as major donors frequently leverage their standing to advocate publicly for the organization, attract additional philanthropic support, and expand the organization's network of potential partners and supporters.

Importantly, many major donors adopt strategic, long-term approaches to their philanthropy. Rather than episodic or spontaneous giving, they often carefully plan their contributions, considering long-term impacts, sustainability, and organizational stability. They may also utilize advanced philanthropic vehicles, such as donor-advised funds, endowments, planned gifts, charitable trusts, or foundations. This forward-looking, strategic mindset aligns closely with nonprofit organizations aiming for sustained, long-term programmatic growth and systemic change.

In addition to their strategic orientation, major donors typically possess an informed, sophisticated understanding of the nonprofit sector and philanthropy's role in addressing complex societal challenges. Many are well-versed in the best practices of nonprofit governance, management, accountability, and evaluation. Their informed perspective encourages organizations to maintain rigorous standards, transparency, and professionalism, raising the bar for organizational effectiveness and accountability.

Furthermore, major donors often seek recognition and acknowledgment for their generosity, though preferences for recognition vary significantly. Some prefer public recognition—such as naming opportunities, public acknowledgment in publications, or award ceremonies—while others favor quiet, anonymous giving. Understanding each donor's specific recognition preferences is essential for nonprofits to tailor stewardship practices appropriately, thereby reinforcing satisfaction and continued engagement.

Finally, major donors demonstrate characteristics of loyalty and consistency, often giving repeatedly to their preferred causes over several years or even decades. Building trusting relationships through careful stewardship, consistent communications, and personalized acknowledgment encourages this ongoing generosity. Nonprofits cultivating loyal major donors benefit from sustained financial stability, deeper partnerships, and a reliable base for future growth and planning.

In conclusion, major donors are characterized by significant financial capacity, deep personal passion for their chosen causes, a strong desire for meaningful engagement, a preference for measurable and impactful outcomes, substantial social and professional influence, strategic and long-term philanthropic thinking, sophisticated understanding of philanthropy, individualized recognition preferences, and a willingness to engage in sustained, loyal relationships. Nonprofits that understand these characteristics can effectively foster rewarding relationships with major donors, resulting in transformative changes.

Recruiting Major Donors

Recruiting major donors is a critical task for nonprofit organizations, necessitating a methodical and carefully structured approach. An effective major donor recruitment process involves several sequential stages: careful identification, strategic research and qualification, thoughtful cultivation, appropriate solicitation, and diligent stewardship. Each stage is crucial to creating lasting relationships and securing meaningful philanthropic investments.

The first stage, identification, involves developing a robust prospect pipeline. Nonprofit organizations must begin by clearly defining what constitutes a major donor for their organization, considering their specific financial needs and strategic goals. Definitions may vary considerably among organizations, but typically, major donors are those capable of contributing substantial gifts significantly above average annual contributions. With clear criteria established, the nonprofit should systematically compile a list of potential donors from various sources. These may include existing donor lists, board member referrals, alumni networks, local business leaders, community leaders, wealthy individuals publicly known for philanthropy, participants at organizational events, and supporters of similar nonprofits or causes. A nonprofit might also utilize tools and databases that specialize in donor prospecting and wealth screening, effectively identifying potential donors based on wealth indicators, giving patterns, affiliations, and philanthropic interests.

After assembling a preliminary list of prospects, the nonprofit must engage in thorough prospect research and qualification—the second critical stage. This process involves conducting comprehensive research on each potential donor to assess their capacity to give, inclination to support the organization's mission, and existing connections to the nonprofit or similar causes. In-depth research should include reviewing publicly available financial information, professional and personal backgrounds, philanthropic histories, community involvements, affiliations, and known interests or passions. Organizations may leverage dedicated prospect research staff, development teams, or third-party consultants and screening services for comprehensive profiling. Upon completion of this research, nonprofits should score and prioritize prospects based on defined criteria, enabling staff to allocate limited time and resources to the most promising donor opportunities. By strategically prioritizing qualified prospects, organizations increase efficiency and the likelihood of success.

With qualified prospects identified, the nonprofit enters the crucial third stage—cultivation. Cultivation is the relationship-building process in which the nonprofit deepens its connection to prospects by sharing organizational goals, programs, achievements, and future plans. This stage focuses on education, personal connection, trust-building, and inspiration, ultimately positioning the nonprofit as an ideal partner for achieving the prospect's philanthropic objectives. Effective cultivation requires personal attention and consistent engagement over a sustained period—often months or years. Nonprofit leaders, senior staff, board members, or influential volunteers should personally reach out to prospects, initiating conversations about shared values, inviting them to exclusive organizational events, providing tours or behind-the-scenes experiences, and involving them in volunteer or advisory capacities. The goal is not yet to directly request a gift but rather to build rapport, foster trust, understand the prospect's motivations, and articulate clearly how the organization's work aligns with their philanthropic interests.

As the relationship deepens and mutual understanding emerges, the nonprofit progresses to the fourth critical stage—solicitation. This stage involves requesting a major contribution from the donor, typically in person through a carefully planned, personalized solicitation meeting. Prior to solicitation, the nonprofit should carefully strategize regarding who will make the ask, the amount to request, the appropriate timing, and the specific project or initiative for which funding is requested. An effective solicitation is informed by a clear understanding of the donor's interests, philanthropic priorities, and capacity gained during cultivation. During solicitation meetings, nonprofit leaders must present a compelling, personalized case for support, clearly articulating how the proposed gift will directly contribute to achieving meaningful outcomes aligned with the donor's values and vision. This discussion should be positive, respectful, and authentic, clearly demonstrating both the urgency of the request and the tangible impacts that the gift can produce. The donor should leave the meeting inspired, confident, and fully informed about the organization's vision, strategy, and expected outcomes.

Following a successful solicitation, or even if the initial response requires further reflection, the nonprofit must prioritize diligent stewardship—the fifth essential stage. Stewardship involves maintaining and deepening relationships with donors after the gift is secured, demonstrating transparency, accountability, and genuine gratitude for their contributions. Effective stewardship practices include timely and personalized thank-you communications, formal gift acknowledgment letters, detailed reporting on the impact and outcomes achieved through the gift, personalized updates and communications, invitations to exclusive events, opportunities for further engagement, and recognition consistent with the donor's preferences. Stewardship ensures donors feel valued, understand clearly how their generosity is advancing the organization's mission, and encourages ongoing involvement and future contributions. By emphasizing robust stewardship, organizations build lasting relationships that foster donor retention, loyalty, and increased philanthropic investment over time.

Beyond these core stages, several additional considerations and best practices contribute to an effective major donor recruitment process. Nonprofits should recognize that major donor cultivation and solicitation requires significant time, effort, and strategic planning; therefore, organizations must invest in dedicated staff, appropriate training, and sufficient resources to execute the major donor strategy effectively. Often, executive directors, CEOs, senior development staff, and board members play critical roles in cultivating and soliciting major donors, reflecting the importance of institutional leadership engagement.

Additionally, organizational leadership should regularly evaluate and refine their major donor strategy through continuous learning, feedback, and adaptation. Systematic evaluation of successes and failures at each stage informs improvements and increases effectiveness over time. Leveraging modern technology, such as donor relationship management software, can streamline the major donor pipeline management, enhance communication, track engagement activities, and measure progress toward fundraising goals. These tools support effective donor tracking, relationship management, and accurate reporting, improving organizational efficiency and donor satisfaction.

Furthermore, successful major donor recruitment often involves mobilizing organizational ambassadors beyond internal leadership. Engaged, influential volunteers, satisfied beneficiaries, and enthusiastic current major donors can play significant roles in identifying, cultivating, and soliciting prospective major donors. Such advocates add credibility to the nonprofit's claims, extend the organization's reach, and amplify its message.

Finally, cultivating a culture of philanthropy within the organization itself supports major donor success. Nonprofits should foster an environment where philanthropy is valued, donor relationships are prioritized, and everyone—from frontline staff to board members—understands and participates in advancing fundraising goals. Internal alignment around fundraising priorities, clear and consistent messaging, and organizational commitment to donor relationships enhance nonprofit credibility and strengthen overall fundraising effectiveness.

In summary, recruiting major donors is a structured, multi-stage process that involves systematic identification, rigorous research and qualification, thoughtful cultivation, personalized solicitation, and diligent stewardship. Each stage is essential, and success at each point builds cumulatively toward lasting donor relationships and substantial philanthropic investment. Moreover, effectively recruiting major donors requires dedicated resources, strategic planning, robust technology, continuous evaluation, engaged leadership, influential advocates, and an organization-wide culture of philanthropy. Nonprofits that commit to these principles and practices position themselves for transformative growth and financial sustainability.

EXAMPLE

A prominent example of a major gift fundraising campaign was Harvard University's ambitious capital campaign, publicly launched in 2013, called "The Harvard Campaign." With an original goal of raising $6.5 billion, the campaign was designed to secure transformational gifts from alumni and major donors to support key strategic priorities including financial aid, faculty research, teaching innovation, campus renewal, and interdisciplinary initiatives.

Throughout the duration of this campaign, Harvard engaged in extensive outreach to major donors, alumni, foundations, and corporate partners. Fundraising activities included personalized solicitations, targeted donor events, customized stewardship, and highly visible public communications that emphasized the lasting impact of large-scale philanthropy. One of the signature elements was the focus on donor relationships—Harvard fundraising staff, senior university officials, and faculty leaders worked closely with donors to identify areas of shared vision and passion, resulting in substantial contributions directed toward meaningful projects.

The Harvard Campaign achieved remarkable results, ultimately raising over $9.6 billion by its conclusion in 2018, significantly surpassing the initial target. The campaign attracted several landmark contributions, including major individual gifts in the tens or hundreds of millions of dollars, allowing the university to significantly expand financial aid, launch new academic and research programs, and enhance facilities and infrastructure. Notable gifts included a $400 million donation from philanthropist John Paulson to support Harvard's School of Engineering and Applied Sciences—now known as the Harvard John A. Paulson School of Engineering and Applied Sciences—and a $350 million gift from the Chan family (Gerald Chan) to Harvard's School of Public Health, renamed the Harvard T.H. Chan School of Public Health.

This highly successful fundraising effort exemplifies a well-designed and executed major gift campaign, highlighting the importance of clear vision, compelling storytelling, effective donor cultivation, and strategic relationship management. Such ambitious campaigns not only provide significant resources for organizational priorities but also demonstrate how a structured, relationship-centered approach can inspire donors to give generously, leaving a lasting legacy that shapes the organization's future.

Planned Giving

Planned giving is a crucial and specialized area within nonprofit fundraising, enabling donors to provide support in ways that extend beyond their lifetimes. Through careful estate and financial planning, donors can structure gifts that are larger and potentially more meaningful than their typical annual contributions. These gifts often involve various legal, financial, and tax considerations, making them an important yet complex aspect of nonprofit management. Understanding the nuances of planned giving, particularly the diverse types of planned gifts available, allows nonprofits to build sustainable funding streams, deepen donor relationships, and ensure organizational longevity.

Defining Planned Giving

Planned giving, often referred to as legacy giving or deferred giving, consists of charitable donations structured through estate or financial planning instruments. Unlike immediate cash gifts, planned gifts are typically arranged during the donor's lifetime but are not fully realized until a future date, often upon the donor's death. Planned giving involves considerable donor forethought, where financial advisors and nonprofit employees work together to meet a donor's philanthropic goals.

Nonprofits benefit greatly from planned giving, as it provides a stable, long-term funding source that enhances organizational capacity, facilitates long-range planning, and builds lasting legacies. For donors, planned giving offers potential financial and tax advantages, enhances personal satisfaction, and helps them make a lasting difference in causes they care about deeply.

The most common vehicles used for planned giving include bequests, charitable gift annuities, charitable remainder trusts, charitable lead trusts, life insurance policies, retirement plan assets, real estate, tangible personal property, and donor-advised funds. Each of these vehicles offers unique benefits, but also require a detailed knowledge of the associated tax ramifications.

Donor Motivation for Planned Giving

Understanding donor motivation is fundamental for nonprofit organizations aiming to cultivate meaningful relationships and encourage planned giving. Unlike spontaneous or routine annual gifts, planned gifts frequently arise from deeply personal motivations, shaped by a donor's values, experiences, aspirations, financial circumstances, and vision for a lasting legacy. The primary motivations are as follows:

- *Personal legacy.* Donors often seek to leave a lasting legacy through planned giving, ensuring their values, beliefs, and priorities continue beyond their lifetime. This motivation includes the desire to be remembered positively and to sustain support for organizations and causes they care deeply about.
- *Tax benefits.* Planned giving offers appealing financial incentives, including tax deductions and estate tax savings. Donors can minimize the tax burden on themselves and their heirs, providing significant financial benefits while simultaneously supporting charitable organizations that align with their values.
- *Desire to make a significant impact.* Planned giving empowers donors to make substantial, meaningful contributions that may exceed what they could comfortably donate during their lifetime. This form of giving enables donors to significantly advance the nonprofit's mission, potentially enabling transformative change or sustainable growth.

- *Financial and estate planning goals.* Donors incorporate planned giving strategies to accomplish estate and financial planning objectives, such as managing wealth transfers, providing for family members, and aligning their estate distributions with their personal values and philanthropic priorities.
- *Recognition and stewardship.* Some donors appreciate and seek the recognition, acknowledgment, and stewardship provided by the nonprofit. Planned giving societies, exclusive events, and other forms of acknowledgment help cultivate a sense of belonging, appreciation, and community among dedicated supporters.
- *Gratitude and reciprocity.* Planned giving donors are often motivated by personal gratitude toward a nonprofit that has positively influenced their lives or communities. They feel compelled to give back in recognition of past services, benefits, or experiences provided by the organization.
- *Satisfaction and personal fulfillment.* Donors frequently find emotional fulfillment, satisfaction, and a sense of purpose in planned giving. Knowing their gifts have lasting value and purpose brings joy, comfort, and peace of mind, reinforcing their identity as generous individuals.

Types of Planned Gifts

Understanding the various planned giving vehicles is essential for nonprofits aiming to establish or strengthen planned giving programs. Below are brief summaries of the principal types of planned gifts that nonprofits encounter.

Bequests

Bequests are the simplest and most common form of planned gift, established when donors designate charitable organizations as beneficiaries in their wills or living trusts. This type of donation is discussed at length later in this chapter.

Charitable Gift Annuities (CGAs)

Charitable gift annuities allow donors to transfer cash, securities, or other assets directly to a nonprofit organization in exchange for fixed payments for life. This structured agreement provides donors financial stability and predictable income streams, while simultaneously ensuring that the nonprofit ultimately benefits upon the donor's death.

When donors enter into CGAs, nonprofits typically follow standard gift annuity rates suggested by bodies like the American Council on Gift Annuities. Payments vary according to the donor's age; typically, older donors receive higher annuity payments.

Donors receive immediate tax deductions for a portion of the gift amount and benefit from stable lifetime income, often partially tax-free. After the donor's lifetime, the remainder of the gift passes to the nonprofit organization.

Charitable Remainder Trusts (CRTs)

A charitable remainder trust allows donors to transfer appreciated assets into a trust, avoid immediate capital gains taxes, receive an income stream, and provide a significant future benefit to a nonprofit. CRTs distribute a fixed amount annually to beneficiaries (often the donor or a family member) for life or a specified period (not exceeding 20 years). After that term expires, the remainder goes to the nonprofit.

Charitable Remainder Unitrusts (CRUTs)

Charitable remainder unitrusts (CRUTs) differ slightly, offering variable income payments based on a fixed percentage of the trust's annual value, which can fluctuate according to the trust's asset values each year.

Both CRTs and CRUTs provide donors with immediate charitable deductions, income streams, and capital gains tax benefits. They can effectively manage retirement income and wealth transfer planning.

Charitable Lead Trusts (CLTs)

Charitable lead trusts provide immediate financial support to a nonprofit for a defined period, after which the trust's remaining assets revert to the donor's family or other beneficiaries. These trusts essentially reverse the structure of charitable remainder trusts, serving as a means of reducing gift and estate taxes while supporting nonprofit programs directly and immediately. There are two main types of charitable lead trusts, which are as follows:

- *Grantor lead trust.* Provides donors with an immediate charitable tax deduction but also returns any remaining assets to the donor after the trust period, with tax consequences for the donor.
- *Non-grantor lead trust.* Passes remaining assets to heirs after the term expires, significantly reducing estate and gift tax liabilities.

Life Insurance Policies

Donors can use life insurance policies as planned gifts in two primary ways:

- *Naming the nonprofit as beneficiary.* The donor retains ownership of the life insurance policy but names the nonprofit as the beneficiary. While this method does not typically offer immediate tax benefits, it allows donors to retain policy control and flexibility.
- *Transferring ownership to the nonprofit.* Donors may transfer ownership of a policy directly to a nonprofit, making the nonprofit the policyholder and beneficiary. This option often generates immediate charitable deductions and supports long-term funding goals.

Retirement Plan Assets

Retirement accounts, including IRAs, 401(k)s, and pensions, represent advantageous options for planned gifts. Naming a nonprofit as the beneficiary of retirement assets often provides substantial tax savings, as retirement plans are heavily taxed when inherited by non-spousal beneficiaries.

Donors can designate nonprofits as partial or sole beneficiaries, ensuring that these assets achieve maximum charitable impact rather than being diminished by significant taxes.

Real Estate Gifts

Donors can leave real estate, such as homes, vacation properties, farmland, or commercial buildings, to nonprofit organizations. Gifts of real estate can be structured as outright bequests or through retained life estates, allowing donors to live in or utilize properties until their deaths while enjoying immediate tax deductions.

Gifts of Tangible Personal Property

Donors may contribute personal property such as art collections, antiques, jewelry, vehicles, and other tangible items. These gifts require special care, often necessitating professional appraisals, insurance considerations, and adherence to IRS guidelines to ensure proper valuations and tax deductions.

Donor-Advised Funds (DAFs)

DAFs are charitable giving accounts established within community foundations, financial institutions, or charitable organizations. Donors contribute assets to these funds, receive immediate tax deductions, and retain advisory privileges on fund distributions. While nonprofits do not directly own these funds, nurturing relationships with DAF donors significantly benefits future philanthropic support.

Establishing an Effective Planned Giving Program

For nonprofits, an effective planned giving program is built upon donor stewardship, education, and sound internal management. We expand upon these concepts below.

Donor Stewardship

An effective planned giving campaign begins and thrives with deliberate and meaningful donor stewardship. Stewardship goes beyond simply thanking donors; it involves fostering long-term relationships built on genuine trust, appreciation, and communication. Nonprofits should demonstrate clearly to their donors that they are valued partners in achieving the organization's mission. Personalized acknowledgment, regular engagement, and meaningful recognition through events, legacy societies, or honor rolls can build strong, lasting connections. Additionally, ongoing communication that highlights the real-world impact of planned gifts—sharing stories of beneficiaries and measurable outcomes—reinforces donor satisfaction, deepens relationships, and fosters future giving. Over time, thoughtful stewardship assures donors that their contributions truly matter and that their legacy will be respected, honored, and celebrated.

Education

An essential aspect of successful planned giving campaigns involves educating both donors and internal stakeholders about available giving opportunities. Many donors may not fully understand planned giving options or their potential benefits. Nonprofits can provide accessible, informative resources—including workshops, seminars, brochures, newsletters, webinars, and online resources—to clarify various giving vehicles such as bequests, charitable gift annuities, trusts, and beneficiary designations. This educational outreach demystifies complex financial and estate-planning concepts and emphasizes mutual benefits, such as fulfilling personal legacy aspirations, securing long-term impact, and enjoying tax advantages. Equally important is internal education, ensuring that staff and board members understand planned giving opportunities and feel comfortable discussing them with donors. This comprehensive educational approach empowers donors to make informed philanthropic choices that are aligned with their financial goals and personal values.

Sound Internal Management

An effectively managed planned giving program requires strong internal systems, consistent processes, and coordinated organizational support. Nonprofits must have dedicated personnel or clearly assigned responsibilities for managing planned giving activities, tracking donor relationships, and ensuring timely follow-up. Establishing robust donor management databases and reliable record-keeping practices is crucial for tracking donor intent, maintaining accurate gift documentation, and managing long-term relationships with donors and their families. Policies and procedures should be documented clearly, detailing how planned gifts are accepted, recorded, stewarded, and recognized. Additionally, effective internal management involves transparent financial reporting and accountability—donors want reassurance that their legacy will be professionally managed and will directly support intended organizational goals. By developing and consistently maintaining these strong internal structures, nonprofits foster donor confidence, organizational stability, and sustainable growth of their planned giving programs.

Conclusion

Planned giving is indispensable for nonprofits seeking long-term viability, financial stability, and meaningful donor relationships. Understanding and promoting diverse planned giving options, from simple bequests to sophisticated charitable trusts, empowers organizations to secure enduring legacies. Through thoughtful implementation and strategic management, nonprofits can maximize philanthropic impact, honor donor intent, and ensure sustainable mission delivery for generations to come.

EXAMPLE

A notable real-life example of a nonprofit effectively conducting a planned giving campaign is the American Heart Association's (AHA) Paul Dudley White Legacy Society. Through this carefully structured initiative, the AHA focuses specifically on encouraging and recognizing individuals who commit to planned giving in support of the organization's long-term mission to fight cardiovascular disease and stroke.

The AHA employs a multifaceted approach that is centered on donor stewardship. Members of the society receive personalized acknowledgment and ongoing recognition through exclusive events, newsletters, and public recognition. These stewardship activities foster a sense of pride, connection, and ongoing engagement among donors, clearly communicating the meaningful impact and significance of their planned gifts.

Education is another cornerstone of AHA's planned giving campaign. The organization actively provides clear and comprehensive resources, seminars, and individual consultations that educate donors and prospects about various planned giving options, including bequests, charitable gift annuities, trusts, and retirement asset designations. By simplifying complex financial terms and clearly demonstrating the tangible benefits and lasting impacts of such gifts, the AHA ensures that donors feel confident and informed when making their philanthropic choices.

Finally, the AHA's campaign is supported by sound internal management practices. A specialized planned giving team oversees gift administration, donor stewardship, and communication efforts, maintaining meticulous donor records and relationships. The nonprofit has clear internal policies for managing, documenting, and acknowledging gifts, ensuring transparency, accountability, and long-term trust. Their well-structured internal operations provide stability and ensure effective donor follow-up, further increasing donors' confidence in the AHA's ability to manage and fulfill their philanthropic intentions.

Overall, the AHA's Paul Dudley White Legacy Society illustrates how donor stewardship, strategic education, and strong internal management combine effectively to build a successful and sustainable planned giving campaign.

Bequests

A *bequest* is a gift of personal property, money, or other assets left to someone through a will after the donor's death. It is a specific instruction in a legal document (usually a will) indicating how assets should be distributed upon the individual's passing. Bequests typically fall into one of the following categories:

- *Specific bequest.* A particular item or property is given to a named individual (e.g., a painting, jewelry, or specific sum of money).
- *General bequest.* A gift, typically monetary, comes from the general assets of the estate, rather than a particular item.
- *Residuary bequest.* A gift of whatever remains (the residue) of the estate after all other gifts, debts, taxes, and expenses have been paid.
- *Contingent bequest.* A gift that only occurs if a certain condition is met, such as the beneficiary surviving the testator.

Bequests play a significant role in shaping the financial stability, strategic growth, and long-term planning of nonprofit entities. As planned gifts, they represent an important source of revenue that nonprofits rely upon to advance their missions, sustain operations, and expand their services. The impact of bequests can be transformative, particularly because they often arrive as sizable, unrestricted funds, providing nonprofits with financial flexibility to respond to emerging needs, innovate, or pursue ambitious, long-term objectives.

Nonprofits frequently benefit from bequests in ways that extend far beyond immediate financial assistance. By receiving substantial sums that are typically larger than regular individual donations, organizations gain increased stability, helping cushion them against economic uncertainties or unexpected revenue shortfalls. Such contributions can also foster organizational sustainability by bolstering endowments, enabling investment in infrastructure, technology, or staff training—all critical for operational effectiveness.

Additionally, bequests can signal broader community support and trust, strengthening the nonprofit's reputation and potentially influencing other donors to consider similar gifts. Organizations often leverage the announcement of significant bequests to inspire current supporters, enhance their visibility, and communicate the long-term value and relevance of their work.

However, dependence on bequests can also present challenges. Their timing and amount are inherently unpredictable, complicating budget forecasting and financial planning. To mitigate these uncertainties, nonprofits often balance their dependence on bequests with diverse fundraising strategies, thereby ensuring more predictable cash flows to sustain their core services and programs.

Ultimately, while bequests are inherently unpredictable and require strategic management, their overall impact is overwhelmingly positive, providing nonprofits with critical resources that enable them to thrive, evolve, and continue making meaningful impacts within their communities.

Soliciting Bequests

Nonprofit organizations can significantly increase their likelihood of receiving bequests from donors by cultivating meaningful, trusting relationships and clearly communicating the impact of legacy giving. One fundamental step is raising awareness among supporters about the possibility and importance of bequests, which can be done through targeted communications, newsletters, annual reports, and personal conversations. Organizations can educate donors about the benefits of planned giving by illustrating how their legacy contributions can create a lasting impact on the nonprofit's mission and on the community it serves.

Another critical step involves establishing and actively promoting a well-structured legacy giving program. Such programs generally include clearly defined procedures for making bequests, helpful materials to guide donors and their advisors, and designated staff or volunteers who are trained to sensitively and effectively handle donor questions and intentions regarding planned gifts. Providing accessible and understandable information on how bequests can be structured—such as sample bequest language, different types of legacy gifts, and potential tax implications—helps donors feel more comfortable and confident about including the organization in their estate plans.

Relationship building and stewardship are also essential to successfully attracting bequests. Nonprofits should invest time in building genuine, long-term connections with donors, understanding their values and motivations, and demonstrating authentic appreciation for their ongoing support. Regular interactions, personal acknowledgments, and opportunities for donors to see firsthand how their contributions make a difference are powerful methods for strengthening emotional ties and inspiring deeper commitment. Many donors choose organizations with whom they've built enduring and trusting relationships, underscoring the importance of consistent, respectful, and meaningful engagement.

In addition, creating recognition opportunities specifically tailored for legacy donors, such as establishing special legacy societies or recognition events, helps to acknowledge and honor those who have included the nonprofit in their estate plans. Publicly celebrating these commitments can inspire others to consider similar giving strategies. However, nonprofits must balance recognition with sensitivity, as some donors prefer privacy or anonymity regarding their estate planning intentions.

Finally, consistent internal record-keeping and follow-up practices are essential for effectively managing potential legacy gifts. Nonprofits should keep careful documentation of donor intentions and commitments, periodically confirm and update these records, and ensure ongoing communication and relationship stewardship. Being organized and professional in these interactions instills confidence among donors and their advisors, increasing the likelihood that planned gifts will materialize as intended.

By integrating legacy giving awareness into their overall fundraising strategy, communicating clearly about the impact of bequests, nurturing meaningful relationships, providing valuable guidance and recognition, and diligently tracking and stewarding donor commitments, nonprofits can significantly improve their chances of securing impactful bequests that sustain and expand their missions well into the future.

EXAMPLE

A notable example of a bequest given to a nonprofit is the generous legacy left by Joan Kroc, widow of McDonald's founder Ray Kroc, to the Salvation Army. Upon her passing in 2003, Joan Kroc provided an extraordinary bequest totaling approximately $1.5 billion to the Salvation Army. At the time, this donation was one of the largest charitable bequests ever recorded, significantly transforming the organization's financial landscape and long-term strategic capabilities.

Kroc's bequest was specifically earmarked for establishing community centers across the United States, aimed at promoting health, education, arts, and cultural enrichment in underserved communities. These centers, named the Ray and Joan Kroc Corps Community Centers, have since provided millions of people with essential services such as recreational activities, educational programs, and social support, making a lasting impact on numerous communities.

This remarkable gift illustrates how a single donor's carefully planned and generous bequest can have lasting and transformative implications for a nonprofit's mission and reach, creating an enduring legacy that continues to benefit society well beyond the donor's lifetime.

In-Memory Giving

In-memory giving, sometimes called memorial giving, refers to donations made to nonprofit organizations in honor of someone who has passed away. Donors who give "in memory" typically make their contributions as a way to pay tribute to a loved one or friend, expressing sympathy and condolences to the bereaved family, while simultaneously supporting a meaningful cause or organization that was valued by the deceased or their family.

These types of donations offer an opportunity to create a positive and lasting legacy from a person's life, highlighting their values, interests, and passions. Nonprofits often acknowledge these gifts by notifying family members or loved ones of the donations made in the individual's honor, thereby providing comfort and showing respect to surviving family members.

In-memory giving is a common practice, and many nonprofit organizations actively encourage this type of contribution through clear communication, memorial gift programs, and dedicated recognition mechanisms (such as memorial walls, tribute websites, or special acknowledgment letters). These gifts not only help the organization financially, but also deepen relationships between nonprofits and donors, creating meaningful connections that are rooted in memory, appreciation, and shared values.

Encouraging In-Memory Giving

Nonprofit organizations can encourage in-memory giving by promoting awareness of this donation option, communicating its value to potential donors, and establishing respectful, simple, and sensitive processes for handling memorial contributions. One important step is integrating memorial giving opportunities prominently into their regular communications, including websites, newsletters, annual reports, and social media channels. By clearly explaining how memorial gifts honor loved ones and help sustain the nonprofit's mission, organizations effectively connect with donors' emotional motivations, providing them with a compassionate and meaningful way to express sympathy, gratitude, and respect for individuals who have passed away.

Another crucial step is ensuring the ease and clarity of the giving process. Nonprofits can create dedicated memorial donation web pages or sections on their sites that explain the process clearly, provide straightforward instructions for making memorial donations, and allow donors to indicate the individual they wish to honor, along with family contacts who should be informed about the tribute. Offering customized acknowledgment options—such as letters or cards sent directly to families recognizing the donor's gesture—demonstrates sensitivity and appreciation, which can encourage repeated memorial giving and deeper donor engagement.

Cultivating relationships with funeral homes, hospice providers, churches, and other community organizations can also significantly enhance opportunities for in-memory giving. By developing partnerships and providing these community-based institutions with memorial donation envelopes, informational brochures, or printed materials explaining the importance and process of memorial contributions, nonprofits effectively extend their reach. When funeral homes and other partners distribute materials to grieving families or their communities, they raise awareness among those who may wish to honor their loved ones in a meaningful and lasting way.

Additionally, nonprofits can establish formal recognition mechanisms to honor those remembered through memorial giving. For example, they might create commemorative walls, engraved plaques, or online tribute pages dedicated to individuals who have been memorialized through donations. These gestures highlight gratitude, foster ongoing connections with donors, and encourage future memorial giving. At the same time, organizations should remain flexible and respectful of privacy, as some families may prefer discreet acknowledgments rather than public recognition.

Another important factor is ensuring that donor stewardship practices remain responsive, compassionate, and sensitive. Expressing timely gratitude to memorial donors and informing families about donations received can help strengthen relationships and build goodwill. By carefully managing these interactions, nonprofits demonstrate their appreciation, respect, and care, enhancing their reputation and deepening donors' trust.

Lastly, nonprofits can periodically share stories that illustrate the positive impact of in-memory donations. By showcasing specific examples of how memorial giving has supported meaningful projects, programs, or community outcomes, organizations reinforce the value of this type of gift. These stories resonate emotionally with donors and family members, inspiring others to consider making memorial contributions when the opportunity arises.

In sum, by raising awareness, clearly communicating the value of memorial giving, simplifying the giving process, building strategic community partnerships, recognizing memorial gifts, providing sensitive donor stewardship, and effectively storytelling the impact of such contributions, nonprofits can greatly enhance their efforts to encourage meaningful and lasting in-memory donations.

EXAMPLE

A notable real-life example of a major in-memory gift is the contribution made by businessman and philanthropist Sidney Kimmel to Johns Hopkins University. In 2001, he donated $150 million to Johns Hopkins to support cancer research and patient care, honoring the memory of his close friend who had died from cancer. Motivated by the loss and his desire to fight cancer through research and treatment, Kimmel's gift established the Sidney Kimmel Comprehensive Cancer Center at Johns Hopkins.

The center became a pioneering institution dedicated to innovative cancer research, comprehensive patient care, and leading-edge clinical trials, significantly enhancing the university's capacity to make groundbreaking advances in oncology. This in-memory gift provided substantial financial resources that helped Johns Hopkins attract leading researchers and clinicians, invest in advanced technologies, and significantly expand its cancer research programs, thereby transforming both cancer care and research outcomes.

This major memorial donation not only honored the personal loss Kimmel experienced but also left a powerful legacy benefiting generations of patients and families. It underscores how impactful in-memory giving can be, illustrating the intersection of personal tribute and profound social impact.

Corporate Giving

Corporate philanthropy is a significant aspect of modern business, with companies donating billions of dollars annually to nonprofit organizations. While these contributions are often framed as altruistic, they are typically driven by strategic motivations that align with business objectives. Corporations donate to nonprofits for various reasons, including enhancing their public image, fostering community engagement, improving employee morale, and gaining financial benefits. Below, we explore the key motivations behind corporate donations.

Enhancing Corporate Reputation and Brand Image

One of the primary reasons corporations donate to nonprofits is to improve their public image. Consumers today are increasingly conscious of a company's social and ethical stance, often choosing to support brands that demonstrate corporate social responsibility. By donating to nonprofits, businesses can showcase their commitment to social causes, build goodwill, and differentiate themselves from competitors.

A strong reputation for philanthropy can also help companies recover from negative publicity. When faced with scandals or ethical controversies, corporations may strategically donate to social causes to rebuild public trust. This form of damage control can improve brand perception and help restore customer loyalty.

Strengthening Community Relations

Companies depend on the communities in which they operate, and supporting local nonprofits fosters positive relationships with residents and stakeholders. Donations to local charities, schools, and community organizations demonstrate a corporation's investment in the well-being of the area, helping to create a stable and supportive environment for business growth.

For businesses with a local or regional focus, engaging with nonprofits can strengthen ties with customers, government officials, and community leaders. A company that actively supports community initiatives may receive preferential treatment, such as tax incentives or regulatory leniency, further reinforcing the financial benefits of philanthropy.

Improving Employee Engagement and Satisfaction

Corporate giving also plays a significant role in employee morale and engagement. Workers today, particularly younger generations, are increasingly drawn to employers that prioritize social responsibility. When a company donates to nonprofits or engages in charitable initiatives, it can create a sense of pride and purpose among employees.

Some corporations involve employees in the decision-making process by allowing them to choose which charities receive donations or by matching employee contributions. Others organize volunteer programs, enabling employees to participate in community service during work hours. These initiatives foster a sense of belonging, increase job satisfaction, and improve overall employee retention rates.

Tax Benefits and Financial Incentives

From a financial standpoint, corporate donations can provide tax benefits. In many countries, businesses can deduct charitable contributions from their taxable income, reducing their overall tax burden. While tax incentives alone may not be the sole motivation for corporate giving, they certainly make philanthropy a more attractive option.

Additionally, some corporations establish their own nonprofit foundations to channel charitable contributions strategically. By doing so, they can maintain greater control over how funds are allocated while still benefiting from tax deductions. These foundations often align closely with corporate interests, supporting causes that indirectly benefit the company's long-term growth.

Aligning with Business Strategy and Market Expansion

Corporate donations are often guided by strategic business interests. Many companies direct their giving toward causes that align with their industry, target audience, or market expansion goals. For example, a technology company might fund STEM education initiatives to cultivate a future workforce, while a food company may support hunger relief programs to reinforce its commitment to addressing food insecurity.

In some cases, corporate philanthropy serves as a market entry strategy. Companies expanding into new regions may donate to local nonprofits as a way to establish goodwill, build brand recognition, and foster trust among potential customers. By associating their brand with socially beneficial initiatives, businesses can gain a competitive edge in new markets.

Building Partnerships and Networking Opportunities

Donating to nonprofits can also facilitate valuable business relationships. Many corporate philanthropy initiatives involve collaboration with other businesses, government agencies, and influential nonprofit organizations. These partnerships can lead to new opportunities for business growth, joint ventures, and strategic alliances.

For instance, a corporation that sponsors a nonprofit event may gain access to influential stakeholders, policymakers, or potential investors. By aligning with respected nonprofit organizations, companies can enhance their credibility and strengthen their industry connections.

Conclusion

While corporate donations to nonprofits may appear purely altruistic, they are often driven by a combination of ethical and strategic considerations. Businesses engage in philanthropy to enhance their reputation, foster community relationships, improve employee satisfaction, gain financial benefits, and align with their broader business objectives. As corporate social responsibility continues to gain importance, philanthropy will remain a key tool for companies seeking to balance profit-making with positive social impact.

Types of Support that Businesses Provide to Nonprofits

Businesses support nonprofit organizations in a variety of ways, extending beyond traditional monetary donations. From in-kind contributions and volunteer programs to corporate sponsorships and pro bono services, companies leverage their resources to help nonprofits achieve their missions. These forms of support not only strengthen nonprofit organizations but also benefit businesses by enhancing their reputation, fostering community engagement, and boosting employee morale. By offering financial aid, expertise, and other resources, businesses play a crucial role in driving social impact and creating meaningful change. The more common forms of support provided by businesses are as follows:

- *Monetary donations*. Businesses often provide direct financial contributions to nonprofits in the form of one-time gifts, annual donations, or multi-year grants. These funds help nonprofits cover operational costs, expand programs, and invest in new initiatives. Large corporations may also establish corporate foundations that distribute grants to organizations aligned with their philanthropic goals.
- *In-kind donations*. Instead of giving money, companies may donate goods or services that support a nonprofit's mission. This can include office supplies, food, medical equipment, technology, or professional services such as legal, marketing, or IT support. In-kind donations help nonprofits reduce costs while gaining access to valuable resources that might otherwise be unaffordable.
- *Employee volunteer programs*. Many companies encourage their employees to volunteer with nonprofits by organizing community service days or offering paid time off for volunteering. Some businesses also establish skills-based volunteering programs, where employees use their expertise to assist nonprofits with specialized projects. These initiatives strengthen employee engagement while providing nonprofits with additional manpower and expertise.
- *Matching gift programs*. Some businesses match their employees' charitable donations, doubling or even tripling the impact of individual contributions. This type of support incentivizes employees to give to nonprofits while ensuring that the organization receives additional funding. Matching gift programs also demonstrate a company's commitment to philanthropy and social responsibility.
- *Corporate sponsorships*. Companies frequently sponsor nonprofit events, fundraisers, or community initiatives in exchange for brand visibility and recognition. Sponsorships can include financial contributions, in-kind support, or promotional assistance. This mutually beneficial arrangement helps nonprofits raise funds while giving businesses marketing opportunities and a positive public image.
- *Cause-related marketing*. Businesses may partner with nonprofits to launch cause-related marketing campaigns, where a portion of sales from a product or service is donated to a charitable cause. These campaigns help raise awareness and funding for nonprofits while allowing businesses to align their brand

with social impact. Consumers often respond positively to these initiatives, making them a strategic marketing tool.

- *Pro bono services.* Companies with specialized expertise, such as law firms, consulting agencies, or marketing firms, may offer their services to nonprofits for free. Pro bono support allows nonprofits to access professional assistance that would otherwise be costly, improving their operations and impact. This type of support also strengthens relationships between businesses and the nonprofit sector.
- *Workplace giving campaigns.* Some businesses facilitate employee giving by setting up payroll deduction programs or fundraising drives within the workplace. Employees can contribute a portion of their salary to a nonprofit of their choice, making charitable giving easy and consistent. Workplace giving campaigns help nonprofits secure steady funding while fostering a culture of philanthropy among employees.
- *Board membership and leadership support.* Business leaders and executives often serve on nonprofit boards, providing strategic guidance, fundraising connections, and leadership expertise. These partnerships benefit nonprofits by giving them access to corporate networks and decision-making experience. At the same time, executives gain personal fulfillment and opportunities for community engagement.
- *Facility and resource sharing.* Some companies allow nonprofits to use their office space, conference rooms, or equipment for free or at a reduced cost. This type of support helps nonprofits save money on operational expenses, allowing them to allocate more resources to their programs. Access to corporate facilities can also enhance a nonprofit's ability to host events, meetings, and training sessions.

EXAMPLE

A notable example of corporate support for a nonprofit is Starbucks' partnership with Feeding America, a nationwide network of food banks. Through its *FoodShare* program, Starbucks donates surplus, unsold food from its stores to local food banks, helping to combat food insecurity and reduce food waste. The initiative ensures that fresh food—including sandwiches, salads, and other perishable items—is safely collected and distributed to communities in need.

Beyond food donations, Starbucks also provides financial support to Feeding America, helping to expand its reach and improve logistics for food recovery efforts. Additionally, Starbucks employees are encouraged to volunteer at food banks and participate in local hunger-relief initiatives, reinforcing the company's commitment to social responsibility. This partnership benefits both organizations: Starbucks enhances its sustainability and corporate social responsibility efforts, while Feeding America receives vital resources to continue its mission of fighting hunger across the United States.

Planning a Campaign to Approach Businesses for Support

Approaching businesses for support requires careful planning and a strategic approach to build partnerships that benefit both the nonprofit and the company. The main steps involved in this process are as follows:

1. *Define goals and objectives.* A nonprofit must first determine what it hopes to achieve through corporate support, whether it's securing financial donations, in-kind contributions, sponsorships, or volunteer assistance. Clearly defined goals help tailor outreach efforts to attract the right business partners. The nonprofit should also set measurable objectives, such as a target funding amount or the number of corporate partnerships to establish. Understanding the organization's specific needs ensures that businesses see how their contributions will make a meaningful impact. A well-defined campaign plan increases credibility and enhances the likelihood of securing support.

2. *Identify and research potential business partners.* Nonprofits should research companies that align with their mission, values, and target audience. Businesses with a history of philanthropy, corporate social responsibility initiatives, or community engagement are ideal candidates for partnership. Understanding a company's giving priorities, past nonprofit collaborations, and key decision-makers helps tailor the approach effectively. A nonprofit should also assess how the business might benefit from the partnership, such as through brand exposure or employee engagement opportunities. A targeted list of potential business partners ensures a strategic and efficient outreach process.

3. *Develop a compelling proposal.* A strong proposal should clearly articulate the nonprofit's mission, the specific type of support needed, and how the partnership will be mutually beneficial. The proposal should include impact data, success stories, and specific ways the business can contribute, such as sponsorship packages or volunteer opportunities. Customizing proposals to align with each company's values and business goals increases the likelihood of a positive response. Visual elements, such as infographics and testimonials, can make the proposal more engaging and persuasive. A well-structured, professional proposal demonstrates credibility and encourages businesses to take action.

4. *Establish contact and build relationships.* Before making a formal request, nonprofits should establish connections with key business representatives through networking events, LinkedIn outreach, or other types of introductions. An initial meeting or phone call allows nonprofits to gauge a company's interest and present their case in a more personal and engaging way. Building relationships with decision-makers increases trust and opens the door for long-term collaboration. Nonprofits should also be prepared to answer questions and address any concerns businesses may have. A relationship-driven approach helps foster genuine partnerships rather than one-time transactions.

5. *Follow up and show appreciation.* After an initial outreach, nonprofits should follow up with businesses to reinforce their request and address any remaining questions. If a company agrees to support the nonprofit, clear communication about next steps, expectations, and timelines is essential. Once support is received,

nonprofits must express gratitude through thank-you notes, recognition on social media, or impact reports highlighting the company's contributions. Maintaining ongoing communication helps strengthen relationships and increases the likelihood of future support.

Pitfalls of Accepting Corporate Support

While corporate partnerships can provide significant benefits to nonprofit organizations, they also come with potential risks. Nonprofits must carefully evaluate the ethical, reputational, and operational implications of accepting business support to ensure that the partnership aligns with their mission and values. Below are some of the common pitfalls that nonprofits may face when engaging with corporate donors.

Reputational Risks and Misalignment of Values

One major risk of corporate support is partnering with a business that does not align with the nonprofit's values or mission. If a company has a history of unethical practices, environmental harm, or labor violations, a nonprofit may face backlash for associating with them. This can lead to a loss of credibility, donor trust, and public support.

For example, in 2018, the National Rifle Association faced public pressure as several companies, including Delta Airlines and Hertz, severed their partnerships following a mass shooting incident. While this case primarily involved companies distancing themselves from a controversial nonprofit, it also highlights how associations with certain businesses can become problematic for nonprofit entities. If a nonprofit is seen as benefiting from a corporation with a negative public image, it may face similar scrutiny and backlash.

Loss of Independence and Mission Drift

Corporate donors may attempt to influence a nonprofit's programs, priorities, or messaging to align with their own interests. This can lead to "mission drift," where the nonprofit shifts its focus away from its core objectives to satisfy a corporate sponsor. In extreme cases, this can undermine the organization's integrity and effectiveness.

For instance, if a health-focused nonprofit receives funding from a fast-food chain, the company may pressure the nonprofit to downplay issues related to unhealthy eating habits. This conflict of interest can weaken the nonprofit's ability to advocate for its mission authentically. To avoid this, nonprofits must set clear boundaries and ensure that corporate contributions do not compromise their goals.

Short-Term Support Without Long-Term Commitment

Some businesses may engage in philanthropy for publicity rather than a genuine commitment to the cause. A nonprofit may receive a one-time donation or sponsorship, only for the company to withdraw support once the marketing benefits have been achieved. This can leave nonprofits in a vulnerable financial position, especially if they have come to rely on the funding.

For example, in some cases, businesses have initiated high-profile cause-related marketing campaigns, pledging a portion of their sales to a nonprofit. However, after an initial promotional period, the company discontinues the campaign, leaving the nonprofit without sustained support. To mitigate this risk, nonprofits should seek long-term partnerships and diversify their funding sources.

Ethical Concerns and Greenwashing

Some businesses use nonprofit partnerships as a way to improve their public image without making meaningful changes to their own practices—a tactic known as "greenwashing" or "cause-washing." In these cases, a company may donate to an environmental or social cause while continuing practices that contribute to the very problem they claim to address.

A well-known example is the controversy surrounding oil and gas companies supporting environmental nonprofits while simultaneously engaging in activities that contribute to climate change. For instance, BP has funded conservation initiatives while facing criticism for its role in major oil spills and continued fossil fuel extraction. Nonprofits must carefully vet corporate donors to ensure that their support is not being used as a public relations tool that contradicts the organization's mission.

Restrictions and Conditional Funding

Some corporate donations come with strict conditions, limiting how the nonprofit can use the funds. While some restrictions may be reasonable, others may force nonprofits to allocate resources in ways that do not align with their priorities. This can reduce a nonprofit's flexibility and ability to respond to urgent needs.

For instance, a company might offer funding only for specific programs rather than general operational costs, making it difficult for the nonprofit to cover essential expenses such as staff salaries or administrative needs. To prevent this issue, nonprofits should negotiate the terms of corporate support and seek unrestricted funding whenever possible.

Conclusion

While corporate support can provide valuable resources and opportunities for nonprofits, it is essential to approach partnerships with caution. Reputational risks, mission drift, short-term commitments, greenwashing concerns, and restrictive funding conditions can all pose challenges. By conducting thorough due diligence, setting clear boundaries, and prioritizing long-term sustainability, nonprofits can maximize the benefits of corporate partnerships while minimizing potential pitfalls.

Fundraising from Foundations

Nonprofits often seek funding from foundations to support their programs, operations, and long-term sustainability. *Foundations* are charitable entities that provide grants to organizations that are aligned with their mission and funding priorities. Unlike individual donations or government funding, foundation grants are typically competitive, requiring nonprofits to submit proposals that demonstrate their impact, financial need, and alignment with the foundation's goals. The main types of foundations are described next.

Private Foundations

Private foundations are typically established by individuals, families, or corporations to distribute charitable grants. They are funded by a single source, such as an endowment from a wealthy donor or a corporation's profits. Private foundations must distribute a minimum percentage of their assets each year to maintain their tax-exempt status. These foundations often have specific focus areas, making it essential for nonprofits to align their proposals with the foundation's mission. Examples include the Gates Foundation and the Ford Foundation.

Corporate Foundations

Corporate foundations are funded and operated by businesses as a way to give back to the community. Unlike private foundations, which rely on an endowment, corporate foundations often receive annual contributions from the parent company. Their grant-making priorities frequently align with the company's values, industry, or geographic footprint. Some corporate foundations favor projects that engage employees or enhance corporate social responsibility goals. Examples include the Coca-Cola Foundation and the Walmart Foundation.

Community Foundations

Community foundations pool donations from individuals, families, and businesses to support charitable initiatives within a specific geographic area. They often provide funding to local nonprofits through competitive grant programs or donor-advised funds. Because they serve a defined region, community foundations prioritize projects that directly benefit their communities. Nonprofits seeking grants from community foundations should demonstrate a strong local impact and connections within the area. Well-known examples include The Chicago Community Trust and the Silicon Valley Community Foundation.

Family Foundations

Family foundations operate similarly to private foundations but are overseen and funded by a single family. The funding priorities often reflect the philanthropic interests of the founding family members. Family foundations may be more flexible and personal in their grantmaking process, with some offering less bureaucratic application procedures. Relationships and networking play a significant role in securing funding from family foundations, making personal connections a valuable asset. Examples include the Walton Family Foundation and the Rockefeller Brothers Fund.

Operating Foundations

Unlike grantmaking foundations, operating foundations primarily use their funds to run their own programs rather than award external grants. However, some operating foundations offer limited grant opportunities to nonprofits that align with their mission. These foundations focus on specific issues such as education, healthcare, or scientific research. Nonprofits interested in securing funding from operating foundations should ensure that their work complements the foundation's existing initiatives. The Carnegie Endowment for International Peace is an example of an operating foundation.

Government-Linked Foundations

Some foundations are affiliated with government agencies and distribute public or private funds to nonprofits. These foundations often focus on policy-driven initiatives, such as economic development, education reform, or environmental sustainability. While they may function similarly to private foundations, their funding sources and priorities are often influenced by government regulations and objectives. Examples include the National Endowment for the Arts and the National Science Foundation.

Each type of foundation has distinct characteristics, funding priorities, and application processes. Nonprofits should research potential funders carefully to ensure alignment with their mission and funding needs.

The Grant Cycle Used by Nonprofits

Foundations follow a structured grant cycle to ensure that funding is distributed effectively to nonprofit organizations that align with their mission and priorities. Understanding this cycle helps nonprofits prepare strong applications and time their submissions strategically. While specific timelines and processes may vary by foundation, the typical grant cycle consists of the stages described in this section.

Before issuing grants, foundations engage in strategic planning to define their funding priorities. This process involves assessing community needs, reviewing past grant impact, and aligning funding with the foundation's mission. Foundations may also revise their focus areas, set new funding goals, or adjust eligibility criteria at this stage. Nonprofits should monitor foundation updates to stay informed about any changes in funding priorities.

Once priorities are set, the foundation formally announces its funding opportunities. This may come in the form of a Request for Proposals, grant guidelines published on the foundation's website, or direct invitations to apply. The announcement typically includes details on funding focus areas, eligibility requirements, application deadlines, and the evaluation criteria that will be used to assess proposals. Some foundations have rolling deadlines, while others have specific grant cycles with annual or biannual deadlines.

During the application phase, nonprofits prepare and submit their proposals according to the foundation's guidelines. Applications often require a detailed project description, goals and objectives, a budget breakdown, an explanation of how the grant will be used, and evidence of the nonprofit's capacity to execute the project successfully. Some foundations also request letters of intent (LOIs) as a preliminary step before inviting full proposals. LOIs serve as brief summaries that help foundations determine which nonprofits should move forward in the process.

After the submission deadline, the foundation begins reviewing grant applications. The evaluation process varies, but typically includes an internal review by program officers and an external review by advisory committees or subject-matter experts. Reviewers assess applications based on factors such as alignment with the foundation's mission, potential impact, organizational capacity, sustainability of the project, and financial feasibility. Some foundations conduct site visits or interviews with applicants to gain a deeper understanding of the proposed initiative.

Once the evaluation process is complete, the foundation's board or grant committee makes final funding decisions. Selected nonprofits receive formal award notifications, which may come with specific terms and conditions regarding fund usage, reporting requirements, and project implementation timelines. Foundations that decline applications may provide feedback to unsuccessful applicants, although this is not always guaranteed.

After accepting the grant, the nonprofit begins implementing its funded project according to the approved plan. Funds may be distributed in a lump sum or in installments, depending on the foundation's policies. Some funders release payments upon meeting specific milestones or demonstrating progress. Nonprofits must carefully manage grant funds to ensure compliance with the foundation's expectations.

Foundations typically require grantees to submit progress reports outlining how funds are being used and what impact the project is achieving. Reports may be required quarterly, annually, or at project completion. Funders use these reports to track effectiveness, measure outcomes, and ensure accountability. Some foundations also conduct site visits or request financial audits to verify that funds are being used appropriately.

At the end of the grant cycle, foundations and grantees assess the success of the funded project. Nonprofits that have demonstrated strong impact and alignment with the foundation's mission may be invited to apply for renewal funding. If renewal is not an option, the foundation and nonprofit close out the grant, ensuring that all reporting and compliance requirements are met.

Understanding the typical grant cycle allows nonprofits to plan effectively, align their proposals with foundation expectations, and strengthen their chances of receiving funding. By pursuing researching grant opportunities, maintaining relationships with funders, and fulfilling reporting requirements, nonprofits can build long-term partnerships with foundations and secure sustainable funding for their missions.

Best Data Sources for Researching Foundations

Finding the right foundations to pursue for grants is crucial for nonprofits seeking funding. Various data sources provide detailed insights into grant opportunities, funder priorities, and past giving trends.

Below are some of the best data sources that nonprofits can use to identify and research potential foundations:

- *Foundation Directory Online (FDO)*. Foundation Directory Online (FDO) is one of the most comprehensive databases for grant research. It provides access to over 100,000 U.S.-based foundations, including grant amounts, past recipients, funding priorities, and application guidelines. FDO allows nonprofits to search by keyword, subject area, geographic focus, and funding history to find the best-aligned grant opportunities.

- *Grants.gov*. For nonprofits seeking government grants, Grants.gov is the primary source of information. Managed by the U.S. federal government, this platform provides a centralized database of funding opportunities from agencies like the Department of Health and Human Services, the National Endowment for the Arts, and the Department of Education. Nonprofits can filter grants by category, eligibility, and funding agency, making it easier to find relevant opportunities.

- *GrantStation*. GrantStation provides a user-friendly platform for nonprofits to research grantmakers, access funding alerts, and use strategic grant-seeking tools. It covers private foundations, government agencies, and corporate giving programs. Nonprofits with a membership can access in-depth profiles of funders, including contact details and funding trends.

- *The Chronicle of Philanthropy*. The Chronicle of Philanthropy is a valuable resource for staying updated on trends in grantmaking and nonprofit funding. While it is primarily a news source, it also publishes reports on major foundation grants, emerging funding priorities, and best practices for nonprofit fundraising.

- *Local community foundations*. Many cities and regions have community foundations that provide grants to local nonprofits. Organizations like the Chicago Community Trust, the New York Community Trust, and similar entities across the country offer funding and capacity-building opportunities. Researching local community foundation websites or reaching out directly can reveal lesser-known but highly accessible grant opportunities.

- *State and regional grant directories*. Many states have nonprofit associations or grant directories that compile funding opportunities specific to a region. Websites like the Minnesota Council on Foundations or Philanthropy California provide curated lists of funders interested in supporting local initiatives. These directories are particularly useful for smaller nonprofits with region-specific missions.

- *Corporate philanthropy and CSR reports*. Many corporations have philanthropic divisions that provide grants to nonprofits, particularly in areas related to corporate social responsibility (CSR) priorities. Reviewing CSR reports, company websites, and platforms like Double the Donation can help identify corporate grant opportunities. Companies like Walmart, Google, and Bank of America have established grant programs that nonprofits can tap into.

- *IRS tax exempt organization search*. The IRS provides a free database where nonprofits can search for tax-exempt organizations, including private foundations. By reviewing 990-PF forms, nonprofits can identify foundations that have awarded grants to similar organizations in the past. This data can help refine grant-seeking strategies by focusing on funders with a proven interest in a nonprofit's mission area.

Successful grant-seeking requires a combination of strategic research and persistence. By leveraging these data sources, nonprofits can identify the best foundations to target, tailor their proposals effectively, and increase their chances of securing funding. Regularly monitoring these platforms and staying informed about grant trends will help organizations build strong, sustainable fundraising strategies.

Why Grant Applications Fail

The following are among the most common reasons why a grant application might fail:

- *Misalignment with the foundation's mission and priorities*. Foundations have specific focus areas, such as education, healthcare, or environmental conservation. If a nonprofit applies for a grant that does not closely align with these priorities, the application is unlikely to be successful. Even if a nonprofit's work is valuable, foundations prefer to fund organizations that directly support their strategic goals.

- *Weak or unclear proposal writing*. A poorly written or disorganized proposal makes it difficult for funders to understand the project's purpose and impact. If the language is too vague, technical, or lacks a logical structure, the reviewer may lose interest. Strong proposals present a compelling case with clear, concise, and persuasive writing that highlights the nonprofit's mission and goals.

- *Lack of demonstrated impact or measurable outcomes*. Foundations want to fund projects that produce tangible, measurable results. If a nonprofit fails to provide clear data, benchmarks, or success stories, funders may doubt the project's effectiveness. A strong application includes specific goals, a plan for tracking progress, and evidence of past achievements.

- *Incomplete or noncompliant applications*. Many applications are rejected simply because they do not follow the foundation's guidelines. Missing documents, exceeding word limits, or failing to meet submission deadlines can lead to automatic disqualification. Carefully reviewing the application requirements and double-checking for completeness is essential before submission.

- *Unrealistic budget or financial instability*. A budget that lacks detail, overestimates costs, or seems unrealistic raises concerns for funders. Foundations want to see that a nonprofit can responsibly manage grant funds and sustain the project beyond the grant period. Financial instability, such as significant debt or dependence on a single funding source, may signal a high-risk investment to funders.

- *Lack of organizational capacity or experience.* Funders want assurance that a nonprofit has the staff, infrastructure, and expertise to execute the proposed project effectively. If an organization lacks a track record of managing similar initiatives, the foundation may question whether it can deliver results. Providing examples of past successes and strong leadership can help build confidence in the nonprofit's ability.

- *Overreliance on one-time grant funding.* Foundations prefer to support projects that have long-term sustainability beyond their initial funding. If a nonprofit does not outline a plan for securing future funding, funders may hesitate to invest. Demonstrating diverse revenue streams, partnerships, or other funding sources can strengthen an application.

- *Poorly established relationships with the funder.* Grantmaking is not just about submitting an application—it also involves building relationships with foundations. If a nonprofit applies for funding without prior engagement, such as attending events or speaking with program officers, the application may not stand out. Strong relationships can help nonprofits better understand funder expectations and increase their chances of success.

- *High competition for limited funds.* Even well-crafted proposals can be rejected due to the sheer volume of applicants. Some foundations receive far more applications than they can fund, forcing them to make difficult choices. In these cases, nonprofits should remain persistent, seek feedback, and continue applying to multiple funding sources.

By avoiding these common mistakes and refining their approach, nonprofits can improve their grant-writing success and build stronger partnerships with funders.

Summary

This chapter explored key fundraising strategies, including direct response fundraising, major gift fundraising, planned giving, bequests, and corporate giving. Nonprofits utilize direct response methods such as direct mail, email, and telemarketing to drive immediate donor action. Major gifts play a crucial role in securing significant financial support, while planned giving and bequests provide long-term sustainability through estate planning and legacy contributions. Additionally, corporate giving offers opportunities for funding, sponsorships, and in-kind donations that align business interests with nonprofit missions. By leveraging these diverse approaches, organizations can strengthen donor relationships and ensure financial stability for their causes.

Tip: For many of the types of fundraising described in this chapter, it can make sense to incorporate a QR code into the fundraising materials sent to donors. With a simple scan using a smartphone camera, supporters can instantly access a donation page, which facilitates immediate donations. QR codes can be placed on a wide range of materials, making them highly versatile for fundraising campaigns. For example, non-profits can incorporate QR codes into printed materials (such as brochures, posters, and business cards), digital platforms (such as websites, social media costs, and email newsletters), and live events (such as banners and T-shirts).

Chapter 7
Donor Retention and Development

Introduction

This chapter explores the critical issue of donor retention, highlighting the challenges and strategic solutions for maintaining long-term donor engagement. While donor acquisition often takes center stage, this chapter emphasizes that retaining existing donors is essential for financial stability and mission success. Key factors contributing to donor attrition include inadequate communication, lack of personalized engagement, donor fatigue, and ineffective stewardship. In the following pages, we discuss best practices for improving retention, such as relationship-building, strategic communication, and leveraging technology for data-driven donor engagement. By adopting a comprehensive approach to donor retention, nonprofits can secure sustained financial support and enhance their long-term impact.

The Problem with Donor Retention

Donor retention remains one of the most significant and persistent challenges faced by nonprofit entities today. While attracting new donors often receives considerable attention, the issue of retaining existing donors frequently gets overshadowed, despite its vital importance to organizational sustainability. Nonprofits rely on consistent, recurring financial support to effectively execute their missions, yet the vast majority of organizations struggle to keep donors engaged over extended periods. The failure to retain donors not only impacts immediate financial stability but also undermines the potential for long-term growth and influence.

There are many reasons behind donor retention challenges. One of the primary underlying issues is that many nonprofit organizations disproportionately focus their resources and attention on donor acquisition. Driven by a persistent need to expand funding sources and reach fundraising targets, organizations often dedicate significant effort and financial resources to outreach efforts aimed at attracting new donors. While acquiring new supporters is undeniably important, the emphasis placed on new donor recruitment frequently diverts attention and resources away from nurturing existing donor relationships. Consequently, established donors may begin to feel undervalued or overlooked, leading them to lose interest, reduce their contributions, or terminate their support altogether.

Additionally, donor retention problems can arise from inadequate or ineffective communication practices. Meaningful, ongoing communication with donors is essential for establishing trust, reinforcing connections, and keeping donors informed about the organization's activities, successes, and challenges. However, many nonprofits fail to establish a consistent and personalized approach to communicating with their donor base. Generic, infrequent, or overly solicitous communications can frustrate donors, diminishing their sense of connection and emotional engagement with the nonprofit.

Moreover, poor acknowledgment practices further exacerbate donor dissatisfaction. Donors frequently report feeling unappreciated or unnoticed after making financial contributions, which significantly undermines their willingness to continue giving.

Another critical factor contributing to poor donor retention is the lack of personalized donor engagement. Donors increasingly seek meaningful, personalized experiences with the organizations they support. However, many nonprofits rely on standardized mass messaging strategies that fail to recognize individual donor interests, motivations, or preferences. The absence of tailored interactions makes donors feel distant from the cause, leading to weakened emotional connections and diminished donor loyalty. Without personalized engagement, donors perceive their contributions merely as transactional exchanges rather than meaningful investments in social change, prompting them to withdraw their support over time.

The complexity of today's donor landscape further complicates retention efforts. Donors are increasingly discerning and sophisticated, with high expectations regarding transparency, accountability, and measurable impact. Many donors now expect to see tangible evidence of their contribution's direct impact and effectiveness in addressing social or environmental problems. When nonprofits are unable or unwilling to clearly communicate their impact, or if they fail to measure outcomes transparently and effectively, donors become skeptical and hesitant. This skepticism inevitably contributes to donor attrition. Furthermore, in a highly competitive nonprofit environment where donors have numerous opportunities to direct their contributions elsewhere, organizations that fall short in demonstrating meaningful impact face significant retention challenges.

Donor fatigue also emerges as a critical challenge to retention. Nonprofits often depend heavily on repeat contributions from a core group of dedicated supporters, particularly in challenging financial environments or in response to pressing societal issues. Repeated appeals, continuous solicitations, and frequent fundraising events can overwhelm or exhaust donors over time. When donors feel consistently pressured for additional funds or perceive constant solicitations as intrusive or burdensome, donor fatigue can set in, causing previously loyal supporters to reduce or eliminate their contributions entirely.

Further complicating the issue of donor retention is the insufficient use of technology and data analytics by many nonprofit organizations. Nonprofits often lag behind the private sector in employing sophisticated data-driven insights and analytics to inform strategic donor engagement practices. Robust data analysis enables organizations to understand donor behaviors, preferences, motivations, and giving patterns. Without these insights, nonprofits rely on guesswork or intuition in donor engagement, leading to inefficiencies and misaligned communications. Lack of technical infrastructure or expertise prevents nonprofits from adopting more sophisticated donor relationship management systems, exacerbating retention problems by undermining strategic relationship-building efforts.

Leadership turnover within nonprofit organizations further compounds donor retention challenges. Donors frequently forge personal connections with key organizational leaders or development staff. Leadership transitions can disrupt these critical relationships, leading to donor uncertainty or distrust. Without appropriate succession planning or clear communication during periods of leadership transition, donors may become detached or disillusioned. The absence of continuity in stewardship practices or organizational vision can negatively influence donors' willingness to continue supporting the nonprofit during and after such transitions.

In addition to these internal organizational factors, economic downturns or uncertainty can severely impact donors' financial capacities and willingness to commit to long-term giving. During periods of economic strain, donors may prioritize personal financial obligations or reduce discretionary charitable giving. Nonprofits that fail to anticipate economic fluctuations and adjust their fundraising strategies accordingly risk losing previously reliable donors. Furthermore, during economically challenging times, organizations that neglect relationship cultivation and rely solely on transactional fundraising tactics struggle more acutely with donor retention.

In summary, donor retention represents a critical yet frequently overlooked challenge for nonprofit organizations. This problem arises from a combination of factors including disproportionate emphasis on donor acquisition, ineffective communication strategies, lack of personalized engagement, donor fatigue, inadequate transparency and impact reporting, technological deficiencies, leadership instability, and external economic pressures. By addressing these underlying challenges, nonprofit entities can significantly improve their donor retention rates, secure long-term financial stability, and enhance their capacity to achieve meaningful, lasting societal impact.

Building Donor Retention

Nonprofit organizations must consistently prioritize donor retention as a key aspect of their fundraising strategy. One essential step toward improved donor retention is to invest deliberately in cultivating strong personal relationships with donors. Rather than viewing donors simply as financial contributors, organizations should see them as valuable partners who are deeply invested in their mission. This means allocating time and resources to regularly engage donors on a personal level. Executive directors, board members, or dedicated donor relations staff should strive to build individualized connections with donors by making periodic phone calls, setting up informal meetings, or sending personalized notes acknowledging milestones or personal life events. Knowing key donors personally and acknowledging their unique interests, motivations, and preferences builds emotional bonds, loyalty, and a sense of personal ownership over the organization's successes.

Tailoring communication to donors' specific interests and giving history is another effective strategy. Organizations can enhance donor retention significantly by customizing messages that directly reflect each donor's individual impact and areas of passion. For example, if a donor regularly supports youth education initiatives within the nonprofit, communications should specifically highlight achievements and developments in educational programs. The deliberate use of segmented donor databases and personalized communication—through letters, emails, newsletters, and social media—makes donors feel uniquely appreciated and reinforces the tangible connection between their contributions and meaningful outcomes.

Regular and transparent communication about the impact of donations is essential in nurturing ongoing donor relationships. Donors naturally want reassurance that their generosity produces meaningful results. Nonprofits should inform donors about how their contributions are specifically benefiting programs, communities, and individuals. Detailed impact reports, compelling stories of beneficiary successes, updates on progress, and testimonials from beneficiaries directly show donors the transformative power of their generosity. When donors can clearly visualize the positive outcomes generated by their support, they are much more likely to remain engaged and to continue contributing.

Proactive stewardship is another fundamental element for enhancing donor retention. Stewardship practices go beyond simple acknowledgment and gratitude. Nonprofits must ensure that every donor receives prompt and sincere thank-you messages immediately after making a donation. For major gifts, personal calls from organizational leaders expressing heartfelt gratitude often prove particularly impactful. Furthermore, nonprofits should provide consistent stewardship over the donor lifecycle by regularly communicating updates, inviting donors to exclusive events or activities, and periodically acknowledging donors' long-term commitment. Special touches, such as sending anniversary thank-you letters commemorating a donor's multi-year engagement or offering exclusive access to behind-the-scenes experiences, make donors feel deeply valued and respected.

Creating meaningful opportunities for active donor involvement in organizational activities is also a powerful retention mechanism. Donors who actively participate in an organization's work tend to become personally invested in its success and longevity. Nonprofits can invite donors to participate in various meaningful ways: joining advisory councils, attending community volunteer days, serving on event committees, or assisting with fundraising campaigns. Direct involvement gives donors firsthand experience with the mission's tangible impacts, strengthens their emotional connections, and fosters ongoing commitment. This participation helps donors see themselves as integral partners rather than passive observers.

Recognizing and celebrating donors' generosity meaningfully and publicly also enhances retention. While some donors prefer anonymity, most appreciate genuine recognition. Nonprofits should regularly acknowledge donors in ways that align with their personal preferences, such as through annual reports, newsletters, websites, or at special events and ceremonies. Organizations might also establish formal recognition programs, such as donor walls, legacy societies, or honor rolls highlighting sustained commitment and loyalty. Public appreciation reinforces donor satisfaction, pride, and motivation, thereby deepening their resolve to continue their support over time.

Responsiveness to donor inquiries, questions, and feedback is another critical factor influencing donor retention. Organizations that make themselves readily accessible, quickly addressing donors' questions or concerns, inspire trust, confidence, and satisfaction. Staff members responsible for donor interactions should receive proper training to provide prompt and respectful responses to every communication received from donors. Nonprofits must also actively seek donor feedback through surveys, informal conversations, and structured interviews. Valuing donor insights and demonstrating sincere willingness to incorporate their suggestions into organizational operations shows respect, deepens donor trust, and fosters a culture of mutual collaboration and long-term engagement.

Transparency and accountability in all financial and operational practices significantly influence donor retention. Today's donors increasingly expect transparency in how their contributions are managed, allocated, and utilized. Organizations should provide clear, concise, and easily accessible financial reports and annual impact assessments. Explaining clearly how donated funds directly support mission-related programs reassures donors that their gifts are being utilized responsibly. Moreover, organizations must openly acknowledge challenges or setbacks, sharing candidly how these issues are being addressed. Genuine transparency and accountability strengthen donor trust, reassuring them that their support contributes meaningfully toward shared goals.

Nonprofits also must carefully monitor, measure, and continually improve their donor retention strategies. Regularly tracking donor retention rates helps organizations understand where improvements are needed and identifies patterns indicating donor dissatisfaction or attrition. By employing data analytics and donor feedback, nonprofits can pinpoint which donor groups are most at risk of disengaging and implement targeted interventions. Regular strategy reviews, donor database assessments, and internal staff training programs enhance retention capacity and ensure that the organization's donor-focused practices remain relevant, effective, and responsive.

Finally, nonprofits should invest consistently in staff training and professional development that is focused explicitly on donor relations, stewardship, and retention strategies. Staff members play a critical frontline role in building and maintaining donor relationships. Empowering them with the skills, resources, and tools needed to nurture meaningful donor engagement significantly enhances overall retention outcomes. By ensuring every staff member understands their vital role in donor satisfaction and engagement, nonprofits can cultivate a culture that deeply values long-term donor relationships.

In conclusion, donor retention requires strategic action across multiple facets of organizational operations. Nonprofits dedicated to cultivating meaningful donor relationships, delivering tailored communication, demonstrating accountability and transparency, thoughtfully stewarding their supporters, inviting active participation, offering genuine recognition, responding promptly to feedback, and continuously monitoring and improving their strategies will position themselves to sustain long-term donor support, strengthen their mission's impact, and achieve lasting success.

Attracting the Right Types of Donors

Identifying new donors who are most likely to evolve into long-term supporters is a critical challenge and an important strategic priority for nonprofit organizations. While attracting donors broadly is valuable, targeting prospects who demonstrate characteristics predictive of lasting engagement can dramatically enhance fundraising stability and impact. Specific steps can be taken to identify and cultivate these potential long-term donors. This process involves an analysis of past donor behavior, precise profiling, strategic prospecting, the effective use of technology and analytics, relationship-building from the outset, and rigorous evaluation.

The first step in effectively identifying promising long-term donors involves closely examining an organization's existing donor base and historical donation patterns. Nonprofits can begin by analyzing data to determine common attributes among current long-term donors, including demographic information such as age, location, occupation, and educational background. Additionally, examining psychographic details like interests, values, giving motivations, and behavioral indicators such as frequency, consistency, size, and method of donation can provide valuable insights. Through detailed donor segmentation and profiling, nonprofits can identify the attributes that correlate most significantly with long-term giving. These insights will form a predictive framework, enabling the organization to seek out new prospects who share these characteristics, thereby increasing the likelihood of successfully converting initial donors into loyal, committed supporters.

Once key attributes of current long-term donors are understood, nonprofits can strategically deploy various prospect research tools to locate new potential donors who match these identified profiles. Prospect research involves the careful investigation and evaluation of potential donor candidates to determine their alignment with organizational values and priorities. For example, nonprofits might utilize databases, professional networks, social media platforms, and publicly available records to identify individuals who have previously supported similar missions or who demonstrate significant philanthropic interests consistent with their own. Publicly available information about personal giving histories, event attendance, board memberships, volunteering commitments, professional affiliations, and even media coverage can help nonprofits build comprehensive and accurate prospect profiles.

In conjunction with prospect research, technology and data analytics tools offer powerful capabilities for predictive modeling and the identification of prospects likely to become long-term donors. Leveraging donor management software, fundraising databases, and customer relationship management platforms, nonprofits can aggregate, integrate, and analyze vast amounts of donor information. Predictive analytics algorithms can help identify prospects whose behavior or demographic profiles mirror those of existing loyal donors. These platforms can also quantify and score a donor's likelihood of long-term engagement, facilitating more strategic allocation of resources toward cultivating the most promising prospects. Investing in specialized fundraising analytics tools thus becomes a highly strategic choice, significantly improving a nonprofit's capacity for identifying and engaging ideal donor candidates.

Further, nonprofits can identify potential long-term donors by cultivating relationships through involvement and engagement opportunities from the very outset. Individuals who engage with an organization through personal participation—such as attending special events, volunteering, touring program sites, or serving on committees—often demonstrate deeper initial interest and investment. Inviting prospects to participate directly, even prior to soliciting financial support, allows organizations to gauge authentic enthusiasm, commitment, and alignment with their mission. Early involvement signals meaningful intent and emotional investment, making these individuals significantly more likely to commit to sustained future support. Proactive relationship-building activities allow nonprofits to observe early indicators of prospective donors' genuine interest, responsiveness, and willingness to invest in the organization's cause and programs long-term.

Nonprofits can also establish initial donation opportunities that are strategically designed to attract and identify donors likely to stay engaged over time. Offering convenient, accessible, recurring giving options—such as monthly giving programs, online subscription donation options, or multi-year pledge arrangements—can help nonprofits attract prospects with greater potential for sustained financial commitments. By observing which donors opt into regular, automated giving, the organization gains important behavioral indicators that these individuals view their donations as an ongoing, sustained relationship rather than a single isolated transaction. An early commitment to recurring gifts clearly indicates a predisposition toward long-term engagement, enabling nonprofits to prioritize follow-up interactions and stewardship efforts accordingly.

Another useful approach in identifying donors likely to remain loyal involves testing and observing initial their responsiveness to personalized communication and appeals. Prospects who respond promptly and positively to personalized outreach—such as tailored emails, direct phone calls, handwritten letters, or personal visits—often show higher likelihood of sustained future engagement. Nonprofits can implement deliberate communication testing protocols, assessing each donor's responsiveness to varying forms of outreach. By tracking response rates, openness to dialogue, and receptivity to personalized interactions, nonprofits can effectively evaluate and identify prospects demonstrating high degrees of engagement, affinity, and potential long-term loyalty.

Nonprofits should also systematically collaborate with their existing supporters, board members, and networks to identify promising new donor candidates. Current long-term donors often associate socially or professionally with individuals sharing similar philanthropic values, interests, and capabilities. Organizations can regularly request referrals from existing committed donors, inviting them to suggest friends, colleagues, or professional contacts who may share similar commitments and passion for their cause. Prospective donors identified via personal recommendations are often predisposed to long-term engagement because they already possess an implicit connection through an existing donor, thereby significantly boosting their likelihood of sustained commitment.

Finally, nonprofits must implement an ongoing evaluation and assessment process for their donor identification strategies. Continuous measurement and monitoring of new donor retention rates enable nonprofits to validate their identification methods, refine predictive models, and fine-tune prospecting approaches. Regularly reviewing donor conversion rates—examining how effectively prospects identified as long-term candidates actually become sustained contributors—provides crucial feedback. Nonprofits can adjust their strategies, update predictive models, revise segmentation criteria, and sharpen prospect profiles based on accurate, real-world retention data. Over time, rigorous evaluation practices significantly improve an organization's capacity to identify new donors most likely to commit to long-term support.

In conclusion, systematically identifying prospective donors who demonstrate high potential for long-term commitment is essential for the sustained financial health and impact of nonprofit organizations. By deeply analyzing past donor behavior, strategically conducting prospect research, utilizing advanced analytics and technology tools, cultivating donor relationships through involvement opportunities, strategically offering recurring giving options, testing communication responsiveness, leveraging existing donor networks, and continuously evaluating outcomes, nonprofits can significantly enhance their ability to attract, engage, and sustain donors who become loyal, long-term supporters.

EXAMPLE

A strong example of a nonprofit effectively attracting the right types of donors can be found in the approach taken by Doctors Without Borders (Médecins Sans Frontières, or MSF). This international humanitarian nonprofit is globally respected for providing emergency medical aid to populations affected by conflicts, epidemics, natural disasters, and exclusion from healthcare. Through carefully targeted outreach, clear mission alignment, thoughtful communication, and strategic donor engagement practices, MSF consistently attracts donors whose values align closely with the organization's mission, making these donors particularly likely to remain loyal, committed, and generous over extended periods.

One critical step Doctors Without Borders takes to attract aligned donors is clearly defining, articulating, and consistently communicating their mission and unique value proposition. Their work is anchored in humanitarian medical aid that is delivered independently, impartially, and neutrally to the most vulnerable populations worldwide. By emphasizing their independent and impartial nature and consistently communicating stories from the frontlines—often from conflict zones and crisis areas—MSF appeals strongly to donors who place great importance on global justice, humanitarian aid, public health, and rapid emergency response. The organization's transparent commitment to neutrality and independence resonates deeply with potential donors who value ethical clarity, credibility, and trustworthiness in humanitarian action. By explicitly highlighting and emphasizing these core principles, MSF attracts donors predisposed to long-term support because their personal values directly align with the nonprofit's central identity and approach.

Doctors Without Borders further attracts the right donors through the careful cultivation of transparent, authentic, and emotionally resonant storytelling. Rather than relying solely on generalized appeals, MSF regularly shares compelling and often deeply emotional narratives directly from medical teams working in challenging and remote locations around the world. Through personal stories from doctors, nurses, midwives, and other medical professionals, MSF provides donors with vivid and authentic glimpses into the immediate impact their contributions make. These frontline accounts depict the critical importance of donor support in real-time, showing precisely how contributions translate directly into lives saved, diseases treated, and dignity restored. By clearly illustrating impact through genuine, emotionally charged storytelling, MSF naturally draws donors motivated by compassion, empathy, and a desire to provide tangible humanitarian aid.

In addition to emotionally engaging stories, Doctors Without Borders offers clear, concrete examples of how donated funds are used. Regular newsletters, reports, and communication campaigns emphasize transparency, showing precisely how donor funds directly equip medical teams, provide vaccinations, establish field hospitals, purchase medical supplies, and support emergency medical missions. By openly and transparently sharing budgetary information and offering detailed impact reports, MSF actively attracts donors who appreciate transparency and accountability. These donors often become long-term partners because they trust that their contributions genuinely make a tangible and measurable difference, reinforcing continued support and commitment.

Doctors Without Borders also attracts the right donors by consistently positioning themselves as nonpartisan, objective humanitarian leaders capable of openly criticizing injustices, even in difficult political circumstances. Their willingness to speak candidly about complex humanitarian crises and advocate publicly for policy changes to improve global health aligns closely with donors who appreciate courageous leadership and authentic advocacy. Such positioning often attracts donors who are highly educated, socially conscious, globally minded, and deeply interested in contributing to positive systemic change. These donors typically remain involved and committed over many years, viewing their support as an extension of their personal and professional values.

Moreover, Doctors Without Borders strategically utilizes targeted communications and digital outreach campaigns to reach those donor segments most likely to share their humanitarian values. Through precise use of digital analytics and donor segmentation, MSF identifies individuals who demonstrate past philanthropic support for similar causes, interest in global issues, or professions connected with healthcare, medicine, human rights, or international development. By reaching potential donors through carefully tailored digital messages and segmented appeals, MSF ensures that its communications resonate strongly with audiences predisposed to mission alignment. This targeted approach increases both the effectiveness and efficiency of their donor recruitment, attracting individuals whose philanthropic behaviors and values naturally align closely with the organization's humanitarian mission.

In summary, Doctors Without Borders effectively attracts donors aligned with their humanitarian medical mission through clear mission articulation, authentic storytelling, transparency, strategic monthly giving programs, courageous advocacy, targeted educational engagement, and precise donor segmentation. This approach has enabled MSF to build a highly loyal donor community that is consistently engaged and motivated to provide sustained support, ensuring long-term financial stability and maximizing their global humanitarian impact.

Donor Value

Donor value is a key fundraising concept that refers to the total benefit a donor provides to a nonprofit organization over the lifetime of their engagement, typically measured in financial contributions, loyalty, advocacy, and personal involvement. It encompasses more than just monetary donations, including intangible factors such as the donor's influence, connections, volunteer efforts, and ability to attract other donors. Understanding donor value helps nonprofits recognize that each donor relationship carries different levels of strategic significance, enabling the organization to prioritize resources, time, and effort most effectively.

By assessing donor value, a nonprofit can tailor its standard of donor care. Rather than treating all donors uniformly, effective nonprofits provide varying levels of attention, recognition, stewardship, and personalization based on each donor's overall value to the organization. This approach does not imply treating lower-value donors poorly or neglecting them; rather, it means focusing extra energy, resources, and personalized attention on those donors who bring the greatest sustained benefit to the organization's mission. Such targeted stewardship ensures that high-value donors—those whose contributions significantly impact organizational success—receive the deeper engagement and personalized attention necessary to maintain and grow their support. At the same time, this approach allows nonprofits to efficiently steward lower-value donors using scaled and automated approaches, ensuring they remain informed and connected while managing limited organizational resources effectively.

Determining donor value involves analyzing several important factors beyond merely a donor's financial contribution amount. Financial generosity, frequency of giving, and consistency over time are key indicators of high donor value, but equally important are considerations such as advocacy potential, influence within the community, and willingness to actively promote the organization's mission to others. Nonprofits must assess a donor's potential lifetime value, considering their capacity and likelihood of future increased support, recurring giving commitments, legacy giving opportunities, and non-financial engagement, such as volunteerism, introductions to new donors, or promoting the organization through professional or social networks. By comprehensively evaluating donors according to these dimensions, nonprofits identify those donors who represent substantial strategic value.

Once donor value is assessed, nonprofits can adjust their standards of donor care accordingly, employing a carefully segmented approach that is tailored to the specific value each donor group represents. Donors demonstrating the highest levels of lifetime value and strategic importance require greater, more personalized stewardship and relationship management. For these donors, nonprofits should deliver customized communication, individualized attention, exclusive involvement opportunities, personalized updates, invitations to special events, and direct interactions with senior organizational leadership. These actions convey genuine respect and appreciation for their generosity and sustained commitment, building stronger emotional connections that reinforce loyalty and encourage continued, growing support.

For instance, a high-value donor might receive personal phone calls or handwritten thank-you notes from the executive director after every major contribution, be invited to private events featuring intimate discussions about the organization's impact, or receive customized reports explicitly outlining the difference their generosity has made. Special recognition opportunities—such as membership in exclusive donor societies, naming opportunities, or lifetime giving awards—also reinforce to these high-value donors that their significant contributions are deeply valued. Personalized stewardship at this level helps cultivate emotional bonds and secure sustained, long-term commitment, ultimately maximizing the donor's lifetime value and benefit to the organization.

Mid-level donors, while still critically important, may receive slightly less intensive—but still personalized and thoughtful—care. Nonprofits can use strategic communication that feels individualized but may involve greater reliance on targeted emails, personalized mailings, or invitations to donor appreciation events designed specifically for mid-tier contributors. Mid-level donors benefit from periodic personalized interactions, occasional personal outreach from key staff, and clear, relevant updates on program successes that are funded by their contributions. These gestures reinforce ongoing engagement, nurture relationships, and strategically position mid-level donors for potential future progression to higher giving tiers.

Lower-value donors, who may contribute smaller amounts less frequently or demonstrate less direct engagement, still require respectful, appreciative, and consistent stewardship, but with fewer resources allocated to them individually. Effective nonprofit practice at this level typically involves scalable, cost-effective strategies such as group-oriented email newsletters, digital impact updates, social media communications, and automated acknowledgment letters. Organizations must ensure that lower-value donors feel recognized, informed, and genuinely appreciated, but should allocate fewer individualized staff interactions at this level. This ensures careful and strategic use of limited organizational resources, while maintaining a positive donor experience that is capable of fostering long-term engagement and potential future upgrades in giving levels.

As donor relationships evolve over time, nonprofits must consistently reassess and adjust their standards of donor care according to changing donor value. Regular tracking and analysis of donor giving patterns, response rates, engagement behaviors, and other metrics enable nonprofits to identify when a donor's value may be increasing or decreasing. Nonprofits must remain responsive and flexible, increasing stewardship and personalization when a donor shows increased generosity or heightened engagement, while appropriately adjusting the resource allocation if donor involvement wanes. This continual reassessment helps ensure that donor care remains relevant, impactful, and strategically appropriate at every stage of the donor lifecycle.

However, nonprofits must approach differentiated donor care thoughtfully, balancing the strategic allocation of resources with the ethical obligation to show gratitude, respect, and genuine appreciation to all donors, regardless of giving level. Differentiation in care should never result in disrespect, neglect, or a lack of appreciation for smaller or lower-value donors. Every donor relationship matters, and effective nonprofits understand the potential for donors to grow in their value over time. Even lower-value donors represent important opportunities for future development, referrals, volunteer engagement, and community advocacy. Therefore, nonprofits must adopt strategies that balance efficiency with genuine, respectful appreciation and engagement at every level.

In conclusion, donor value is a vital consideration guiding nonprofits in determining the appropriate level of donor care and stewardship. By strategically differentiating stewardship practices based on comprehensive assessments of donor value—nonprofits can effectively prioritize their resources, maximize donor retention, deepen relationships, and ensure long-term sustainability. This donor-centric approach creates stronger emotional connections, enhances donor loyalty, increases retention rates, and ultimately maximizes the lifetime value each donor provides to the organization.

EXAMPLE

Cedar Hill Community Hospital Foundation serves as the fundraising arm of a regional non-profit hospital system that provides comprehensive medical care, advanced health services, and community wellness programs. The Cedar Hill Foundation periodically calculates donor value, assessing the lifetime potential value that each donor represents to the organization.

To illustrate how Cedar Hill calculates donor value, consider a representative donor named Mrs. Jennifer Thompson. Jennifer made her first contribution five years ago, donating $1,000 following exceptional treatment that her husband received at the hospital. Over the next four years, she contributed annually, with donations varying between $500 and $2,000. She also began volunteering, serving on the hospital foundation's special events committee, and recruited several friends who subsequently became donors.

When Cedar Hill Community Hospital Foundation calculates Jennifer's total donor value, they examine multiple critical elements, including her historical giving behavior, potential lifetime value, non-monetary involvement, and referral value. The initial step involves calculating her historical donor value. In Jennifer's case, Cedar Hill compiles her past giving amounts:

- Year one: $1,000
- Year two: $500
- Year three: $1,500
- Year four: $2,000
- Year five: $1,000

Total historical donor value for Jennifer over five years equals $6,000.

Next, Cedar Hill calculates Jennifer's average annual gift, an important metric often used in estimating future donor value. Over five years, she contributed a total of $6,000, meaning her average annual donation is calculated as:

$$\$6,000 \div 5 \text{ years} = \$1,200 \text{ per year}$$

Having established Jennifer's average gift, Cedar Hill then estimates her potential future lifetime donor value. They consider her age, income, philanthropic propensity, relationship history with the organization, and affinity for their mission. Suppose Jennifer, currently aged 55, expresses ongoing strong interest in the hospital's mission. Cedar Hill estimates conservatively that she may actively support them at a similar rate for at least another 15 years. Using her average annual giving amount of $1,200, they project her potential future contributions as follows:

$$\$1,200 \times 15 \text{ years} = \$18,000 \text{ projected future lifetime value}$$

Combining historical giving ($6,000) with estimated future giving ($18,000), Jennifer's total lifetime monetary donor value is therefore projected at approximately $24,000.

However, the Foundation recognizes that true donor value extends beyond monetary contributions alone. Therefore, they assess and quantify the additional non-financial contributions Jennifer makes, particularly her volunteer service. Over five years, Jennifer volunteers approximately 40 hours per year, totaling 200 hours. Cedar Hill assigns an estimated financial value

112

to volunteer hours using the nationally recognized standard value (e.g., approximately $30/hour, a common value used by nonprofits to reflect volunteer contributions):

200 hours × $30/hour = $6,000 estimated volunteer contribution value

Additionally, Cedar Hill considers the value Jennifer generates through advocacy, referrals, and introductions to other potential donors. Jennifer has referred three new donors to Cedar Hill, each contributing $2,500 in total thus far, totaling $7,500 in referral-based donor value to date. Cedar Hill conservatively estimates Jennifer may continue making occasional referrals in coming years, potentially adding another $5,000 in future referral-based value.

Summing these various elements provides Cedar Hill with a comprehensive calculation of Jennifer's overall donor value, both monetary and non-monetary:

- Historical monetary giving: $6,000
- Projected future monetary giving (next 15 years): $18,000
- Volunteer service value (200 hours): $6,000
- Referral-based giving value (actual and projected): $12,500

This brings Jennifer's total estimated comprehensive donor value to approximately $42,500.

This thorough calculation significantly influences the Foundation's stewardship and donor care strategy for Jennifer. Given her high overall donor value, Cedar Hill provides her with personalized, high-touch donor stewardship, including invitations to exclusive donor events, periodic personal phone calls or visits from senior foundation leadership, and targeted communications tailored specifically to her interests and preferences.

By calculating donor value in this detailed manner, Cedar Hill Community Hospital Foundation strategically identifies donors whose lifetime engagement warrants enhanced attention, personalized stewardship, and additional resources. Such careful calculations of donor value inform strategic planning and resource allocation, guiding the nonprofit's approach to donor relations and ensuring that valuable supporters remain engaged and committed for the long term.

The Donor Communication Cycle

The donor communication cycle is a strategic framework that nonprofit organizations use to guide interactions with donors, aiming to build meaningful, sustainable relationships that maximize donor retention. This cycle consists of a planned series of stages—acknowledgment, education, involvement, solicitation, stewardship, and ongoing evaluation—carefully designed to keep donors engaged, informed, and emotionally invested over time. When nonprofits consistently follow this structured communication cycle, donors feel recognized, valued, and deeply connected to the cause, significantly increasing their likelihood of remaining committed supporters for the long term.

The first phase in the donor communication cycle is the timely acknowledgment of a gift, letting donors know that their generosity is noticed and appreciated.

Timeliness is key; a donor should ideally receive an initial acknowledgment—whether via email, handwritten note, personalized phone call, or combination thereof—within days, or even hours, of their donation. These acknowledgments should be sincere, personalized, and specific, explicitly referencing the donor's name, the amount given, and how the funds will directly support the organization's mission and impact. This immediate response serves as a foundation, establishing a positive emotional connection and demonstrating to the donor that the organization values their generosity and commitment.

Following acknowledgment, the next stage involves ongoing education and information sharing. Effective nonprofits communicate regularly with donors, providing meaningful content that is designed to reinforce their understanding of the organization's mission, impact, and specific programs. Communications at this stage typically take the form of newsletters, impact reports, donor updates, annual reports, and targeted emails, each clearly explaining how donor contributions make tangible differences. Nonprofits should provide stories illustrating the direct benefits and transformational results stemming from donors' gifts. By consistently and transparently informing donors about the outcomes of their generosity, organizations help donors visualize the specific, real-world impact their contributions have, deepening their emotional attachment and encouraging continued investment.

Next, nonprofits move donors into the involvement stage, actively inviting and encouraging them to participate personally in meaningful organizational experiences. Offering opportunities for personal engagement allows donors to become closer to the nonprofit's work, creating direct, emotional bonds with the mission and its beneficiaries. This may include invitations to events, volunteer opportunities, site visits, webinars, interactive virtual experiences, or meetings with organizational leadership and frontline staff. Personal involvement enhances donors' sense of partnership and commitment, helping them perceive themselves as integral stakeholders in the organization's success and sustainability. Encouraging direct experiences cultivates deeper understanding and appreciation, strongly motivating donors to remain involved over the long term.

After donors have been appropriately informed and engaged, nonprofits then strategically enter the solicitation phase. Rather than presenting appeals solely as isolated asks, effective organizations frame solicitations as natural extensions of ongoing, meaningful relationships. Carefully personalized solicitations—based on past giving history, specific areas of donor interest, and established relationships—communicate clearly why continued support matters, connecting emotionally with the donor's own values and personal philanthropic goals. In this stage, nonprofits should offer options that make continued giving convenient and appealing, such as recurring monthly donation plans, multi-year pledges, or designated giving opportunities that are closely aligned with donor passions. Thoughtfully structured solicitations emphasize continuity, trust, and meaningful partnership, reinforcing to the donor the significant ongoing difference their continued support can create.

Following successful solicitations, the donor communication cycle moves into an essential stewardship phase. Stewardship is the ongoing expression of appreciation, gratitude, and recognition that occurs consistently, not only immediately after a donation. It encompasses regular touchpoints, personalized gestures, thoughtful recognition, and expressions of gratitude that reaffirm donors' generosity and their valuable role in organizational success. Effective stewardship might involve sending personalized progress updates, exclusive invitations to special donor appreciation events, or recognition of long-term giving milestones such as donor anniversaries or lifetime contribution levels. Consistently stewarding donors reinforces their sense of belonging, pride, and value within the organization, motivating ongoing loyalty and increased generosity.

Integral to the donor communication cycle is an ongoing evaluation and assessment process. Nonprofits must routinely assess their communication effectiveness by actively gathering donor feedback and measuring donor responsiveness, retention rates, and satisfaction. Periodic surveys, interviews, and informal conversations allow organizations to gain insights directly from donors regarding their communication preferences, satisfaction with stewardship activities, perceived impact, and motivations for continued support. Armed with this feedback, organizations can continuously refine and improve their communication strategies and adjust interactions to better meet donor needs, expectations, and interests.

Successful implementation of the donor communication cycle demands coordinated internal organizational practices. Staff members responsible for donor relationships must clearly understand their specific roles and responsibilities within the cycle, ensuring seamless integration between each stage. Nonprofits should adopt effective data-management practices, using donor relationship management software to systematically track donor engagement, responses, giving history, preferences, and interactions. Data analytics and donor segmentation tools allow nonprofits to customize and personalize communication strategies effectively, ensuring that appropriate content reaches donors at the most relevant and impactful moments.

Ultimately, the donor communication cycle is a strategic and structured approach that nonprofits utilize to cultivate deeper relationships with their supporters. By acknowledging donations, consistently educating donors, actively involving them in meaningful experiences, strategically timing personalized solicitations, carefully stewarding relationships, and continually evaluating and refining their communication practices, nonprofits significantly strengthen their donor connections. Implementing this comprehensive, donor-centered communication cycle enhances donors' satisfaction, fosters genuine emotional attachment, builds trust, deepens long-term commitment, and ultimately maximizes donor retention.

The Donor Pyramid

The *donor pyramid* is a strategic fundraising concept used extensively by nonprofit organizations to structure their donor relationships and plan for gradually escalating donations. At its core, this concept visualizes donor relationships and contributions as a hierarchical pyramid, with lower-level, entry-point donors forming a broad base, mid-level donors positioned in the middle tiers, and fewer—but significantly larger—major donors situated at the top. This visual framework provides nonprofits a valuable tool to clearly segment donors based on their capacity, propensity, and willingness to contribute, enabling focused donor cultivation strategies that are aimed at progressively moving donors upwards through increasingly substantial giving tiers.

Initially, at the bottom tier of the donor pyramid, nonprofit organizations attract the largest number of supporters, typically contributing smaller amounts. These lower-tier donors often come to the nonprofit through broad-based appeals and accessible entry points, including small-scale fundraising campaigns, events, online donation opportunities, and social media outreach. While donations at this level may individually seem modest, these broad-based initiatives collectively create a robust foundation upon which future donor relationships can be cultivated. Nonprofits should consistently engage this tier through regular communication, sincere acknowledgment, and strategic education about the organization's mission, impact, and future opportunities. By keeping entry-level donors informed, recognized, and emotionally connected, organizations set the stage for future increased giving, as these donors gradually become more invested in the organization's success.

As donors become more consistently engaged, nonprofits seek to actively move them upward into mid-level tiers. At this intermediate stage of the donor pyramid, donors generally make fewer but larger gifts, signifying growing commitment and affinity toward the nonprofit's mission. Nonprofits can cultivate these mid-level donors through carefully tailored interactions, personalized stewardship, and targeted opportunities that are designed to deepen donor commitment and involvement. Examples of effective mid-tier cultivation strategies include invitations to special events, exclusive briefings on programs or organizational progress, behind-the-scenes tours, and participation in smaller-group interactions with organizational leadership. At this level, nonprofits also encourage donors to commit to recurring or multi-year giving arrangements, thus stabilizing funding and creating opportunities to demonstrate sustained impact. Through personalized cultivation and more intentional relationship building, mid-level donors increasingly see themselves as integral partners, naturally deepening their emotional commitment and positioning them favorably for progression to higher tiers.

The upper tiers of the donor pyramid, representing major donors and key philanthropic investors, are fewer in number but significantly greater in terms of donation size and impact. At this highest level, donors possess substantial financial capacity and willingness to commit significant funds toward meaningful initiatives that are aligned with their personal values. Nonprofits must identify mid-level donors who have demonstrated consistent interest, loyalty, and capacity, moving them toward this major donor level through strategic outreach. Cultivation at this stage requires highly personalized relationship management. Typically, nonprofit leaders—such as executive directors, board members, or senior development staff—will personally steward relationships with these high-tier donors. Stewardship at this level might include private meetings and customized proposals that align directly with the donor's philanthropic vision, values, and personal legacy goals. Nonprofits often engage these donors in direct conversations about significant and transformative giving opportunities, naming opportunities, planned giving options, and long-term multi-year pledge arrangements, which allow donors to create a lasting impact.

To effectively use the donor pyramid concept in strategic planning, nonprofit organizations must continuously maintain a dynamic and forward-thinking approach, creating pathways that encourage donors to move upward through increasingly significant giving levels. This requires careful planning, research, and relationship management, combined with consistent communication at every tier. Effective utilization of the donor pyramid means segmenting donors based on detailed demographic and psychographic profiles, tracking donor engagement and behaviors, and designing individualized cultivation strategies to encourage upward mobility through the pyramid. Using technology and data analytics, organizations can monitor donor interactions, identify opportunities for escalation, and tailor strategies for specific segments of the donor base, significantly increasing their success in progressively upgrading donors.

Additionally, the donor pyramid concept helps nonprofits clearly see the interdependence between lower-tier and higher-tier donors. While higher-tier donors contribute greater sums individually, these donors often emerge initially from the lower tiers. Without a strong, broad foundation of entry-level donors who can eventually move up, organizations find it challenging to sustain long-term major donor relationships. Therefore, nonprofit organizations must continually invest in robust strategies to attract, retain, and engage donors at all levels, understanding clearly how each tier's cultivation practices ultimately impact upward mobility through the pyramid.

In planning future fundraising initiatives, nonprofit leaders should regularly revisit their donor pyramid, examining donor movement between levels, assessing retention rates, evaluating cultivation success, and identifying areas for improvement. Strategic fundraising planning becomes far clearer and more manageable when seen through the lens of the donor pyramid. Nonprofits can set realistic fundraising goals for each tier, determining precise targets for the number of donors, average donation size, and specific engagement actions necessary to move donors upward. Moreover, this visualization clearly demonstrates fundraising potential, allowing organizations to allocate resources, staff time, and cultivation efforts strategically, maximizing their returns on investment.

Ultimately, the donor pyramid concept provides nonprofits with a practical blueprint for understanding, managing, and actively growing donor relationships. Through consistent donor segmentation, tailored relationship-building, personalized stewardship, intentional cultivation, and regular analysis, nonprofits leverage the donor pyramid to escalate donors to higher levels of giving over time. This structured approach facilitates long-term donor engagement, generates consistent revenue growth, enhances financial sustainability, and maximizes mission impact for the nonprofit organization.

Summary

In conclusion, donor retention poses a persistent challenge for nonprofit organizations, influenced by factors such as ineffective communication, lack of personalized engagement, and donor fatigue. Addressing these issues requires a strategic, data-driven approach that is focused on relationship-building, transparency, and long-term stewardship. By implementing targeted donor engagement strategies and leveraging technology to personalize interactions, nonprofits can significantly improve their donor retention rates and financial sustainability. Ultimately, fostering meaningful donor relationships ensures continued support, enabling organizations to achieve a lasting social impact.

Chapter 8
Fundraising Events

Introduction

Fundraising events play a crucial role in the financial sustainability and growth of nonprofit organizations. Beyond generating revenue, these events create opportunities for donor engagement, brand visibility, volunteer involvement, and strategic partnerships. By hosting fundraising events regularly, nonprofits can strengthen their relationships with supporters while increasing awareness of their mission. This chapter explores the many benefits of periodic fundraising events and provides insights into how they contribute to long-term success.

The Value of Fundraising Events

Fundraising events are a cornerstone of financial sustainability and community engagement for nonprofits. While grants, donations, and membership fees provide vital funding, periodic fundraising events offer unique benefits that extend beyond mere revenue generation. These events create opportunities for donor engagement, brand visibility, volunteer mobilization, and strategic partnerships, all of which contribute to an organization's long-term success. By hosting fundraising events at regular intervals, nonprofits can build relationships with supporters, strengthen their mission impact, and create a sense of community around their cause. We expand upon these concepts below.

Financial Sustainability and Revenue Generation

The most immediate and obvious benefit of running fundraising events is financial support. Nonprofits rely on diverse funding streams, and events provide a direct means of generating revenue. Ticket sales, sponsorships, live auctions, raffles, and merchandise sales are just a few of the revenue-generating opportunities that come with a well-planned event.

In addition to immediate revenue, successful events often lead to long-term financial benefits. Many donors who attend fundraising events later become recurring contributors. Events provide nonprofits with the opportunity to introduce potential donors to their mission in a more personal and engaging way, increasing the likelihood of ongoing financial support.

Furthermore, fundraising events allow organizations to tap into new sources of funding. Companies and local businesses are often willing to sponsor or donate goods and services in exchange for brand exposure at nonprofit events. These sponsorships reduce event costs and boost overall revenue, making fundraising events an effective financial strategy.

Building Stronger Relationships with Donors

Fundraising events create a unique platform for nonprofits to connect with their donors in a meaningful way. Unlike online campaigns or direct mail appeals, in-person and virtual events allow supporters to interact with an organization's leadership, staff, and beneficiaries. This personal connection fosters trust, deepens engagement, and enhances donor loyalty.

When donors attend an event, they have the opportunity to see firsthand how their contributions make an impact. Whether it is through guest speakers, video presentations, or direct interaction with beneficiaries, fundraising events provide a tangible representation of an organization's work. Seeing the real-world effects of their donations makes supporters more likely to continue giving in the future.

Additionally, fundraising events serve as an excellent opportunity to recognize and appreciate existing donors. Acknowledging donors publicly—whether through speeches, awards, or exclusive VIP experiences—makes them feel valued and appreciated. This strengthens their emotional connection to the cause and encourages continued support.

Increasing Brand Awareness and Community Engagement

A nonprofit's visibility is crucial to its ability to attract funding, volunteers, and partnerships. Periodic fundraising events serve as a powerful marketing tool, increasing awareness of the organization and its mission within the community. When a nonprofit consistently holds engaging and well-organized events, it establishes itself as a prominent force in the sector.

Events also generate publicity through various media channels. Local news outlets, radio stations, and online publications often cover nonprofit events, providing free exposure to a wider audience. In addition, social media platforms allow nonprofits to amplify their message, reaching thousands of potential supporters through event promotions, live streams, and post-event highlights.

Moreover, fundraising events bring together diverse groups of people who share an interest in a nonprofit's cause. These gatherings create a sense of community and belonging, which is essential for long-term engagement. Supporters who feel a personal connection to an organization are more likely to advocate for it, spread the word, and recruit others to join the cause.

Attracting and Engaging Volunteers

Volunteers are the backbone of many nonprofit organizations, providing essential labor and support for events and daily operations. Fundraising events offer an excellent opportunity to attract new volunteers while keeping existing ones engaged.

When individuals volunteer at an event, they gain firsthand experience with the organization's mission and work. This exposure often leads to a deeper commitment and ongoing involvement beyond the event itself. Many volunteers who start by helping at fundraising events later become long-term supporters, donors, or even board members.

Additionally, successful fundraising events create a positive and rewarding experience for volunteers. Engaging activities, recognition, and a sense of accomplishment encourage volunteers to stay connected with the organization. When people feel valued and see the impact of their contributions, they are more likely to remain involved over the long term.

Strengthening Partnerships and Networking Opportunities

Nonprofits rely on strong relationships with businesses, community leaders, and other organizations to maximize their impact. Fundraising events provide a natural setting for networking and partnership-building.

Businesses that sponsor or donate to events often become long-term partners, offering additional resources, financial support, and promotional opportunities. Local businesses, corporations, and philanthropic organizations are more likely to invest in a nonprofit if they see its ability to engage the community and produce successful events.

Additionally, fundraising events attract community leaders, policymakers, and influencers who can help advance a nonprofit's mission. By inviting these individuals to participate as speakers, honorary guests, or sponsors, nonprofits can build relationships that lead to future collaborations, advocacy efforts, and funding opportunities.

Educating the Public and Advocating for the Cause

Fundraising events serve as an educational platform, allowing nonprofits to raise awareness about important issues and advocate for their cause. Through speeches, panel discussions, interactive exhibits, and multimedia presentations, organizations can inform attendees about their work and inspire action.

Events also provide an opportunity to dispel misconceptions, share success stories, and highlight the real impact of a nonprofit's efforts. When people leave an event feeling informed and inspired, they are more likely to become advocates for the cause, spreading awareness through word-of-mouth and social media.

Additionally, advocacy-focused fundraising events can mobilize communities around key policy initiatives or social issues. Events like charity runs, rallies, and benefit concerts bring attention to important causes, influencing public opinion and encouraging civic engagement.

Diversifying Fundraising Strategies

Relying solely on one type of fundraising method—such as grants or online donations—can be risky for a nonprofit. Economic downturns, changes in donor behavior, and shifts in funding priorities can all impact a nonprofit's revenue. Hosting periodic fundraising events ensures a diversified income stream, thereby reducing their financial vulnerability.

Events also allow nonprofits to experiment with different fundraising tactics, such as crowdfunding, peer-to-peer fundraising, and hybrid (in-person and virtual) events. By testing new approaches and analyzing their effectiveness, organizations can refine their strategies to maximize future fundraising success.

Additionally, hosting a variety of events—such as gala dinners, charity auctions, fun runs, and benefit concerts—ensures that a nonprofit appeals to a broad audience. Different types of events attract different demographics, allowing organizations to engage supporters of various age groups, interests, and giving capacities.

Creating a Tradition and Legacy of Giving

Annual or recurring fundraising events help establish a sense of tradition, making giving a regular part of supporters' lives. When an event becomes an anticipated community gathering, it fosters long-term engagement and loyalty.

Recurring events, such as an annual gala or charity walk, create a sense of continuity and reliability, encouraging past attendees to return each year. Over time, these traditions strengthen the nonprofit's identity and reputation, making it a trusted and well-known organization within its sector.

Additionally, multi-generational giving can emerge from longstanding fundraising traditions. Families who attend annual events together pass on their commitment to younger generations, ensuring the sustainability of the nonprofit's donor base.

Conclusion

Periodic fundraising events are essential to a nonprofit's success, providing financial stability, donor engagement, increased visibility, and opportunities for advocacy. Beyond raising money, events help build community, foster volunteerism, and strengthen strategic partnerships. By hosting engaging and impactful fundraising events, nonprofits create lasting connections with their supporters, ensuring long-term sustainability and mission impact.

A well-executed event does more than generate funds—it inspires people, strengthens relationships, and advances a nonprofit's cause. When done strategically and consistently, fundraising events become a powerful tool for nonprofits to grow, thrive, and make a lasting difference in the communities they serve.

Types of Fundraising Events

Nonprofits can host a variety of fundraising events to engage donors, raise funds, and promote their mission. Each type of event offers unique benefits and challenges, making it important for organizations to choose the right format based on their goals, audience, and resources. Below are some common fundraising event types, along with their advantages and disadvantages.

- *Gala dinners and banquets.* Gala dinners and banquets are formal fundraising events that typically include a seated meal, entertainment, auctions, and keynote speeches. They provide an opportunity to engage high-net-worth donors and corporate sponsors in an elegant setting. Galas can generate significant revenue through ticket sales, sponsorships, and live auctions. However, they require extensive planning, a large budget, and a strong guest list to be successful. The costs associated with venue rental, catering, and entertainment

can be high, making it critical to ensure a strong return on investment. Additionally, these events may not appeal to younger or lower-income donors.

- *Charity auctions.* Charity auctions involve selling donated items or experiences to the highest bidder, with proceeds benefiting the nonprofit. Live auctions create an engaging atmosphere, while silent and online auctions allow broader participation. These events can attract corporate sponsors and donors willing to contribute valuable items or services. However, securing high-value auction items and ensuring competitive bidding can be challenging. Organizing an auction requires careful planning, from setting up bidding platforms to coordinating logistics for item collection and distribution. Additionally, if bidding is low, the nonprofit may not raise as much as expected.

- *Walks, runs, and bike rides.* Charity walks, runs, and bike rides encourage community participation while promoting health and wellness. These events allow individuals to fundraise through peer-to-peer campaigns, increasing donor engagement. They are often accessible to a broad audience, making them inclusive and highly participatory. However, logistics such as securing permits, coordinating routes, and ensuring participant safety require careful planning. Weather can also impact attendance and overall success, especially for outdoor events. Additionally, these events may not generate as much revenue per participant compared to higher-ticket events like galas.

- *Benefit concerts and performances.* Benefit concerts and performances—such as theater shows, comedy nights, or music festivals—raise funds through ticket sales and sponsorships while providing entertainment. These events can attract a diverse audience and increase awareness of the nonprofit's cause. Partnering with well-known performers or artists can boost attendance and media coverage. However, securing talent, renting a venue, and managing production costs can be expensive. If ticket sales do not meet expectations, the nonprofit may struggle to cover expenses. Additionally, coordinating event logistics and technical requirements can be complex.

- *Golf tournaments and sporting events.* Golf tournaments and other sporting events, such as tennis matches or bowling fundraisers, appeal to corporate sponsors and high-income donors. They provide networking opportunities and allow for significant fundraising through entry fees, sponsorships, and additional activities like raffles. These events often have a high return on investment when well-organized. However, they require securing a venue, recruiting participants, and managing logistics such as tournament scheduling. Weather conditions can also impact outdoor sporting events. Additionally, these events may have a limited audience, primarily attracting individuals who already participate in the sport.

- *Crowdfunding and virtual fundraising events.* Crowdfunding campaigns and virtual events, such as webinars, online challenges, or virtual concerts, leverage digital platforms to raise funds from a wide audience. They offer a cost-effective way to engage donors worldwide, with minimal overhead compared to in-person events. Social media and email marketing can amplify outreach, increasing participation and donations. However, online fundraising can be competitive, requiring strong storytelling and promotional strategies to stand out. Technical challenges, such as platform reliability and audience engagement, may also arise. Additionally, without a personal, in-person experience, some donors may feel less emotionally connected to the cause.

- *Peer-to-peer fundraising campaigns.* Peer-to-peer fundraising encourages supporters to raise money on behalf of a nonprofit by creating personal fundraising pages and asking their networks for donations. This method leverages personal connections, expanding the nonprofit's donor base and increasing community involvement. It is cost-effective, since it relies on existing supporters to promote the cause. However, its success depends on the motivation and outreach efforts of individual fundraisers. Some participants may struggle with fundraising, requiring additional support and resources. Additionally, without proper engagement and follow-up, the nonprofit may not build lasting relationships with new donors.

- *Raffles and sweepstakes.* Raffles and sweepstakes allow participants to enter for a chance to win prizes in exchange for a donation or ticket purchase. These events are easy to organize and can raise funds quickly with minimal upfront investment. They can also be incorporated into larger events, such as galas or auctions, to boost overall fundraising. However, legal regulations regarding gambling and gaming licenses must be considered. Securing attractive prizes is essential to drive ticket sales and engagement. Additionally, raffles alone may not cultivate long-term donor relationships compared to more interactive fundraising events.

- *Community festivals and fairs.* Community festivals and fairs bring together families and local businesses for entertainment, food, games, and educational activities. These events create a strong sense of community and allow nonprofits to engage with a wide audience. Revenue is generated through vendor fees, ticket sales, sponsorships, and merchandise. However, large-scale events require significant planning, permitting, and the coordination of multiple vendors and volunteers. Weather can also impact outdoor festivals, affecting attendance and revenue. Additionally, high logistical costs may reduce overall profitability.

- *Dine-to-donate and restaurant fundraisers.* Dine-to-donate events involve partnering with a restaurant that donates a percentage of sales to the nonprofit on a designated day. These fundraisers require minimal effort from the nonprofit and provide an opportunity for community engagement. They can also be repeated regularly, allowing supporters to contribute simply by dining out. However, the revenue potential is often lower than other fundraising events, as nonprofits typically receive only a small percentage of sales. The success of these events depends on strong promotion and participation. Additionally, restaurant partners may have restrictions on scheduling and contribution amounts.

- *Workshops, seminars, and educational events.* Workshops, seminars, and panel discussions offer nonprofits an opportunity to educate the public while raising funds through ticket sales, sponsorships, or suggested donations.

These events position the nonprofit as a thought leader in its field, enhancing credibility and outreach. They also attract individuals who are genuinely interested in the cause, fostering long-term engagement. However, finding expert speakers and creating compelling content requires planning and effort. Attendance may be limited if the topic is too niche or poorly marketed. Additionally, in-person educational events may have higher venue and logistical costs compared to virtual alternatives.

- *Themed parties and social events.* Themed parties, such as masquerade balls, trivia nights, or holiday celebrations, provide a fun and relaxed way to engage donors while raising funds. These events encourage social interaction and can attract a diverse audience, including younger supporters. Revenue is generated through ticket sales, raffles, sponsorships, and drink sales. However, planning a unique and engaging event requires creativity and attention to detail. The costs of venue rental, entertainment, and decorations must be managed carefully to ensure profitability. Additionally, social events may not always effectively communicate the nonprofit's mission if not well-structured.

Each type of fundraising event offers unique advantages and challenges, making it essential for nonprofits to choose formats that align with their goals, resources, and target audience. Whether hosting a gala, a walkathon, or a virtual campaign, nonprofits can diversify their fundraising strategies to maximize impact and engagement. By leveraging a mix of event types, organizations can build stronger donor relationships, increase financial sustainability, and enhance their community presence.

Why People Attend Fundraising Events

People attend fundraising events for a variety of reasons, ranging from personal connections to the cause to the social and entertainment value of the event itself. Fundraising events provide attendees with an opportunity to support meaningful work while also engaging in enjoyable and memorable experiences. Whether motivated by philanthropy, networking, or simply having a good time, attendees play a crucial role in a nonprofit's success. Below are some of the key reasons why people choose to participate in nonprofit fundraising events.

- *Supporting a cause that they care about.* The most common reason people attend fundraising events is their passion for the nonprofit's mission. Many attendees have a personal connection to the cause, whether they have directly benefited from the organization's work, know someone who has, or simply believe in its impact. Attending an event allows them to contribute financially and show solidarity with the organization's efforts. Seeing firsthand how their contributions make a difference can deepen their commitment and encourage continued involvement.
- *Building and strengthening social connections.* Fundraising events often serve as social gatherings where attendees can connect with friends, colleagues, and like-minded individuals. Whether it's a gala, a charity run, or a benefit concert, these events provide a chance to spend time with others while

supporting a good cause. Many people attend because they were invited by a friend, family member, or co-worker, making it a shared experience. The social nature of these events can create a sense of community and belonging, encouraging repeat attendance in the future.

- *Networking and professional opportunities.* Many fundraising events attract business leaders, community influencers, and philanthropists, making them ideal for networking. Corporate sponsors, professionals, and entrepreneurs attend these events to meet potential partners, clients, or investors while also demonstrating their commitment to social responsibility. High-profile events such as gala dinners, golf tournaments, and business luncheons provide a space for meaningful conversations and professional relationship-building. For some attendees, these events offer the dual benefit of contributing to a cause while also expanding their network.

- *Enjoying entertainment and unique experiences.* Fundraising events often feature high-quality entertainment, performances, guest speakers, or exclusive experiences that attract attendees. Whether it's a live concert, an art auction, or a themed party, the entertainment aspect adds value beyond the philanthropic purpose. Many people attend simply because the event offers a fun and memorable experience. Attendees may also be drawn to unique opportunities, such as meeting celebrities, bidding on exclusive auction items, or participating in special activities that they wouldn't normally have access to.

- *Fulfilling personal or corporate philanthropy goals.* For individuals and companies looking to give back to the community, attending fundraising events is a structured way to fulfill their philanthropic goals. Many businesses encourage employees to participate in charity events as part of their corporate social responsibility initiatives. Some individuals also see these events as a way to contribute to society in a meaningful and visible way. Attending a fundraising event allows them to donate while also engaging with the organization and seeing their impact in action.

- *Recognition and prestige.* Some attendees participate in fundraising events because they offer a level of recognition or prestige. High-profile charity galas, donor appreciation dinners, and exclusive fundraising events provide opportunities for individuals and organizations to be publicly acknowledged for their contributions. Many events recognize major donors through awards, special seating, or public mentions, which can be a motivating factor for those who appreciate acknowledgment. Additionally, some people attend because they want to be associated with a well-respected cause and a prominent nonprofit organization.

- *Participating in a fun and interactive way to give back.* Traditional donation methods, such as writing a check or making an online contribution, can feel impersonal to some donors. Fundraising events provide a more engaging and interactive way to give back. Activities such as charity walks, auctions, trivia nights, and themed parties allow attendees to contribute while also participating in an enjoyable experience. This sense of involvement makes giving feel more rewarding and tangible, increasing the likelihood of continued support.

- *Being inspired by the organization's work.* Many people attend fundraising events to learn more about the nonprofit and its impact. Inspirational speakers, testimonials from beneficiaries, and presentations about the organization's achievements can move attendees to become more involved. Some attendees may not have been previously engaged with the nonprofit but leave the event feeling inspired to volunteer, donate, or advocate for the cause. Events that effectively tell the nonprofit's story and showcase its successes often create lasting emotional connections with attendees.
- *Encouragement from friends, family, or employers.* Peer influence plays a significant role in event attendance. Many people attend fundraising events because a friend, family member, or employer encouraged them to participate. Workplace giving programs, social groups, and community networks often promote nonprofit events, increasing attendance through personal invitations. This word-of-mouth support helps nonprofits attract new donors who may not have been previously aware of the organization or its mission.
- *Tradition and routine giving.* For some attendees, participating in a nonprofit's fundraising events is part of an annual tradition. Many organizations host recurring events, such as annual galas, charity runs, or benefit auctions, that long-time supporters look forward to each year. These traditions create a sense of continuity and reinforce giving as a regular habit. Families, corporate teams, and social groups may make attending certain events a yearly commitment, strengthening their bond with the nonprofit over time.

People attend nonprofit fundraising events for a variety of reasons, including their passion for the cause, social and networking opportunities, entertainment, and the chance to give back in an interactive way. Whether motivated by personal connections, professional interests, or a desire to be part of a community, attendees play a crucial role in a nonprofit's fundraising success. By understanding what draws people to these events, nonprofits can design engaging, meaningful experiences that not only raise funds but also build lasting relationships with supporters.

Factors Driving the Success of Fundraising Events

Fundraising events are a crucial tool for nonprofits to generate revenue, build donor relationships, and increase awareness of their mission. However, not all events achieve their intended goals. The success of a nonprofit fundraising event depends on several key factors, from strategic planning to audience engagement and effective marketing. When these elements are properly executed, they not only maximize financial contributions but also strengthen long-term connections with supporters. Below are the essential factors that contribute to a successful nonprofit fundraising event:

- *Clear goals and objectives.* Establishing specific, measurable goals helps guide planning and execution. Whether the focus is on raising a certain amount of money, expanding donor outreach, or increasing community engagement, having a defined purpose ensures that all efforts are aligned with the nonprofit's mission.

- *Strong event planning and logistics.* Effective event coordination, including venue selection, scheduling, permits, and accessibility, is essential for a seamless experience. A well-organized timeline and contingency plans help prevent last-minute issues and ensure that everything runs smoothly.
- *Targeted audience engagement.* Understanding the target audience and tailoring the event experience to their interests increases participation and donations. Personalized invitations, networking opportunities, and interactive experiences help create a meaningful connection between attendees and the nonprofit's cause.
- *Effective marketing and promotion.* Utilizing a multi-channel marketing approach, including social media, email campaigns, press releases, and influencer partnerships, maximizes event visibility. Compelling storytelling and eye-catching promotional materials attract more attendees and potential donors.
- *Compelling storytelling and mission connection.* Successful events evoke an emotional response by highlighting the nonprofit's impact through testimonials, videos, and speeches. When attendees see tangible evidence of their contributions making a difference, they are more likely to support the cause financially and long-term.
- *Diverse fundraising opportunities.* Providing multiple ways to give—such as ticket sales, live and silent auctions, raffles, sponsorships, and mobile donations—ensures that all attendees can contribute at different financial levels. A variety of fundraising streams increases overall revenue potential.
- *Corporate and community partnerships.* Partnering with businesses, community groups, and sponsors helps reduce event costs while expanding outreach. Sponsors provide financial support, in-kind donations, and promotional assistance, benefiting both the nonprofit and the partnering organization.
- *Volunteer and staff support.* A dedicated team of volunteers and staff is crucial for event success. Well-trained personnel help manage logistics, engage guests, and ensure a smooth operation, enhancing the overall attendee experience.
- *Post-event follow-up and relationship building.* Thanking attendees, donors, and sponsors through personalized messages and impact reports strengthens relationships and encourages future giving. Nonprofits that maintain post-event engagement increase donor retention and build long-term support.

A successful nonprofit fundraising event is built on careful planning, audience engagement, effective marketing, and meaningful storytelling. By focusing on these key factors, nonprofits can create memorable events that not only raise funds but also foster long-term donor relationships. When executed well, fundraising events become powerful tools for sustaining and growing an organization's impact.

Summary

Periodic fundraising events are a vital strategy for nonprofits, offering financial stability, deeper donor engagement, and increased community awareness. Beyond generating revenue, these events create lasting relationships, mobilize volunteers, and strengthen partnerships that sustain long-term impact. Ultimately, a well-executed event does more than raise funds—it builds a legacy of giving and reinforces the nonprofit's role as a force for positive change.

Chapter 9
Measuring Fundraising Performance

Introduction

Tracking nonprofit fundraising performance is crucial for optimizing campaigns, improving donor engagement, and ensuring long-term sustainability. This chapter explores essential indicators, like total funds raised, revenue growth rate, donor retention, and acquisition costs, providing insights into how organizations can optimize their strategies. By tracking these metrics, nonprofits can make data-driven decisions to improve sustainability and maximize their fundraising potential.

Revenue Metrics

There are several valuable metrics associated with the revenue generated by a nonprofit, focusing on the gross amount raised, the rate of growth, the average donation size, whether revenue is recurring, and whether it is restricted or unrestricted. The key factors associated with each one are noted below.

Total Funds Raised

Total funds raised is the total amount of money a nonprofit collects through various fundraising efforts within a specific timeframe. This includes individual donations, grants, corporate sponsorships, event revenue, and other contributions. Tracking this metric helps nonprofits evaluate their financial health and fundraising effectiveness. It provides a clear picture of how well the organization is meeting its revenue goals, and can serve as a benchmark for future growth. The key factors influencing total funds raised are as follows:

- *Fundraising channels used.* Revenue depends on the mix of online donations, direct mail, major gifts, events, grants, and corporate sponsorships.
- *Donor acquisition and retention.* A strong donor base, with high retention rates and repeat giving, contributes to sustained fundraising success.
- *Fundraising strategies and campaign performance.* Effective campaigns, peer-to-peer fundraising, and matching gifts can significantly boost the amount of funds raised.
- *Economic and external factors.* Economic downturns, policy changes, and global events can impact donor willingness to give.

Revenue Growth Rate

The revenue growth rate measures the percentage increase (or decrease) in a nonprofit's fundraising revenue over a given period—typically year-over-year or quarter-over-quarter. It helps organizations assess their financial health, track fundraising effectiveness, and set realistic growth goals. The key factors influencing the revenue growth rate are as follows:

- *Donor retention and acquisition.* A high donor retention rate increases repeat giving, stabilizing revenue growth. Also, a steady pipeline of new donors ensures sustainability and offsets donor churn.
- *Fundraising campaign performance.* Well-planned annual giving campaigns, events, and peer-to-peer fundraisers can drive revenue spikes, while digital fundraising enhances donor engagement.
- *Recurring and major gifts.* Growth in monthly recurring donations provides a predictable income stream.
- *Economic conditions and external factors.* Economic downturns can reduce disposable income, which affects donation levels. In addition, government policies, tax incentives, and social issues may influence donor behavior.
- *Operational efficiency.* Strong donor stewardship and relationship-building foster continued giving, while efficient cost management ensures that fundraising expenses do not outpace revenue gains.

Average Gift Size

The average gift size is a key fundraising metric that measures the average amount donated per transaction within a specific timeframe. It helps nonprofits understand whether donors tend to give small but frequent donations or larger one-time gifts. In addition, comparing average gift sizes across different campaigns (e.g., direct mail vs. online giving) helps identify which strategies drive higher-value contributions. The key factors influencing the average gift size are as follows:

- *Donor type and giving capacity.* Major donors tend to increase the average gift size, while small individual donors may lower it.
- *Fundraising channel used.* Online giving usually results in smaller, more frequent donations, while direct mail appeals can generate mid-sized gifts from loyal donors, and major gift campaigns often yield the highest donation amounts.
- *Suggested giving levels.* Providing suggested donation amounts (e.g., $50, $100, $250) can influence donor decisions.
- *Recurring vs. one-time donations.* Recurring donors typically give smaller amounts per transaction, lowering the average gift size. Conversely, one-time large gifts significantly raise the metric.
- *Economic factors.* Economic downturns may lead to smaller donations.
- *Donor engagement.* Well-nurtured donors often feel a stronger connection to the cause and may increase their giving over time.

Recurring Donation Revenue

Recurring donation revenue is the total amount of funds a nonprofit receives from donors who give on a regular, automated basis - usually monthly, quarterly, or annually. These donations come from committed supporters who set up recurring payments, ensuring a steady stream of income for the organization. This is an important metric, because recurring donations create a reliable revenue stream, allowing nonprofits to plan budgets, allocate resources, and sustain long-term programs with greater confidence. Also, recurring donors typically contribute more over time than one-time donors, increasing their overall financial impact. In addition, retaining donors is cheaper than acquiring new ones, so recurring giving programs enhance fundraising efficiency by reducing marketing and outreach expenses. The key factors influencing recurring donation revenue are as follows:

- *Number of recurring donors.* The more donors enrolled in a recurring giving program, the greater the revenue impact.
- *Average recurring gift size.* Higher monthly or quarterly donation amounts lead to increased revenue.
- *Donor retention.* The longer donors continue their recurring contributions, the more valuable they become. High churn (drop-off) rates can significantly reduce overall revenue.
- *Ease of sign-up.* A seamless donation process (including credit/debit cards, Venmo, ACH transfers, and digital wallets) increases sign-ups and reduces barriers to entry.
- *Ongoing engagement.* Regular communication, appreciation, and impact updates encourage donors to continue giving and potentially increase their contribution amounts.

Restricted vs. Unrestricted Funds

The restricted vs. unrestricted funds metric is a crucial financial indicator that nonprofits track to ensure financial flexibility while honoring donor intent. It measures the proportion of restricted (designated for specific programs or purposes) versus unrestricted (available for general use) funds within total fundraising revenue. This is an essential metric to monitor, because unrestricted funds allow nonprofits to cover operational expenses (salaries, rent, utilities) and invest in organizational growth. Conversely, a heavy reliance on restricted funds can create financial strain if a nonprofit's core costs are not adequately funded. The key factors influencing the proportion of restricted to unrestricted funds are as follows:

- *Donor preferences.* Major donors, corporate sponsors, and grantmakers often provide restricted funds. Individual donors are more likely to give unrestricted funds, especially for general appeals.
- *Grant and foundation funding.* Many foundations require nonprofits to use grants for specific projects, increasing the proportion of restricted funds.
- *Fundraising messaging.* Campaigns focused on general support (e.g., "Support Our Mission") tend to raise more unrestricted funds. Conversely, program-specific appeals (e.g., "Fund Scholarships for Low-Income Students") typically generate restricted donations.

- *Government funding.* Government funding is often highly restricted, allocated for specific services or projects.
- *Donor education.* Educating donors about the importance of unrestricted gifts can encourage more flexible contributions.

Donor Metrics

There are several essential metrics associated with the donor base of a nonprofit, focusing on the donor retention rate, acquisition cost, lifetime value, churn rate, and the number of new donors. The key factors associated with each one are noted below.

Donor Retention Rate

The donor retention rate is the percentage of donors who continue to give to a nonprofit from one year (or period) to the next. This is an important metric, because acquiring new donors is significantly more expensive than retaining existing ones. Studies suggest it costs 5–7 times more to acquire a new donor than to keep an existing one. Also, loyal donors tend to increase their giving over time, making them a more stable revenue source. Furthermore, repeat donors are more likely to become brand ambassadors, spreading awareness and bringing in new donors. The key factors influencing donor retention are as follows:

- *Personalized donor stewardship.* Sending timely and heartfelt thank-you messages and acknowledging past contributions helps to retain donors.
- *Transparent reporting.* Providing clear reports on how funds are making a difference (impact stories, financial reports).
- *Consistent engagement.* Regular updates through newsletters, social media, and personalized emails, as well as inviting donors to events, webinars, or exclusive Q&A sessions with leadership.
- *Ease of giving.* Encouraging monthly giving programs, which retain donors at a higher rate.
- *Recognizing loyalty.* Highlighting long-term donors in annual reports, social media, or donor walls.
- *Sending follow-ups.* Sending reminders to past donors who have not given recently, as well as conducting lapsed donor surveys to understand why they stopped giving.

Donor Acquisition Cost

Donor acquisition cost measures the average cost to acquire a new donor. It helps organizations evaluate the efficiency of their fundraising efforts and determine the sustainability of their donor growth strategies. This is important, because an excessively high acquisition cost can lead to the financial ruin of a nonprofit. The key factors influencing donor acquisition cost are as follows:

- *Marketing methods*. Different acquisition strategies come with varying costs. Digital ads tend to be lower-cost but require ongoing optimization, while direct mail and events are often higher-cost but may yield higher-quality donors.
- *Target audience*. Highly engaged donor demographics (e.g., mission-driven younger donors) may have a lower acquisition cost, while harder-to-reach or high-net-worth individuals may require costlier outreach.
- *Brand awareness*. Well-known nonprofits benefit from lower donor acquisition costs due to strong credibility and word-of-mouth referrals, while newer or smaller organizations often face higher acquisition costs, since they must build trust from scratch.
- *Donor retention*. A high donor acquisition cost is acceptable if the lifetime value of a donor is also high. Or, if donors churn quickly, the organization will continuously spend on acquisition, increasing their overall fundraising costs.
- *Campaign efficiency*. Poorly targeted ads, inefficient messaging, or low-converting donation pages can inflate the donor acquisition cost. A/B testing, personalization, and better donor segmentation can lower the donor acquisition cost by increasing conversion rates.

Lifetime Value of a Donor

The lifetime value of a donor is an estimate of the total revenue that donors are expected to contribute over their entire relationship with an organization. The lifetime value concept helps nonprofits make informed decisions about donor acquisition, retention strategies, and resource allocation. The key factors influencing donor lifetime value are as follows:

- *Donor retention rate*. The longer a donor continues giving, the higher their lifetime value. High retention means strong relationships and consistent engagement with donors.
- *Average donation amount*. A higher lifetime value is often linked to donors who give larger gifts over time. Cultivating mid-level and major donors can significantly boost the overall lifetime value of all donors.
- *Frequency of giving*. One-time donors have a much lower lifetime value when compared to recurring donors.
- *Major gift giving*. Planned giving (wills, estate gifts) significantly raises the overall donor lifetime value.

Donor Churn Rate

Donor churn rate is the percentage of donors who stop giving to a nonprofit over a specific period, typically measured annually. It is a critical metric, because high donor churn means a nonprofit is constantly replacing lost donors instead of building long-term, sustainable support. A high churn rate makes it difficult to grow, as nonprofits must acquire new donors just to maintain their existing funding levels. In addition, acquiring new donors is significantly more expensive than retaining existing ones. The key factors influencing donor churn rate are as follows:

- *Lack of engagement.* If donors feel unappreciated or disconnected, they are less likely to give again.
- *Poor donor experience.* Complicated or inconvenient donation processes can discourage repeat giving, while slow or impersonal acknowledgment of donations can make donors feel undervalued. Further, a lack of transparency on how funds are used may cause donors to lose trust.
- *Economic factors.* Donors may stop giving due to financial hardship or changing priorities.
- *Lack of mission alignment.* If donors no longer feel connected to the nonprofit's cause, they may stop giving.

Number of New Donors

The number of new donors measures how many individuals have contributed to an organization for the first time within a specific period. It reflects an organization's ability to attract fresh support and expand its donor base. Nonprofits rely on a healthy donor pipeline to sustain and expand their operations. A steady inflow of new donors ensures that an organization isn't overly dependent on a small group of repeat contributors. In addition, donor retention rates can be low (often around 40-45% for first-time donors), so acquiring new donors is essential to offset attrition and maintain fundraising levels. The key factors influencing the number of new donors are as follows:

- *Marketing strategies.* A strong website, social media activity, and SEO-friendly content make it easier for potential donors to find and engage with the nonprofit. Further, paid ads (Google Ads, Facebook Ads) and collaborations with influencers or corporate sponsors can increase donor acquisition.
- *Fundraising campaign effectiveness.* Clear fundraising goals, emotional storytelling, and urgency (e.g., limited-time matching gifts) can improve conversion rates.
- *Donation experience.* A simple, mobile-optimized donation form increases the likelihood of conversion, as does accepting multiple payment options.
- *Community engagement.* Fundraising events, volunteer programs, and corporate partnerships can all attract new sponsors.
- *Donor engagement.* Prompt, heartfelt acknowledgments make new donors feel valued and more likely to give again.

Fundraising Campaign Metrics

There are several key metrics associated with fundraising campaigns, focusing on the return on investment, pledge fulfillment rate, and contact response rate. The key factors associated with each one are noted below.

Return on Investment

Return on Investment (ROI) is a key performance metric used by nonprofits to assess the efficiency and effectiveness of their fundraising efforts. It measures how much revenue is generated for every dollar spent on fundraising activities. A high ROI indicates strong financial efficiency, while a low ROI may suggest that too much is being spent relative to the funds raised. A poor ROI outcome can result in funds being shifted to more effective fundraising strategies. The key factors influencing ROI are as follows:

- *Fundraising method used.* Digital campaigns (email, social media) tend to have higher ROI due to lower costs, while events (galas, auctions) often have lower ROI due to high expenses (venue, catering). Major gifts and grants typically yield high ROI, but they require long-term donor cultivation.
- *Donor retention levels.* Acquiring new donors is expensive, which can lower ROI. Retaining existing donors is more cost-effective, leading to higher ROI over time.
- *Campaign effectiveness.* Well-targeted campaigns with strong messaging and donor engagement generate better returns. Conversely, poorly executed campaigns may have high expenses and low conversion rates, thereby reducing ROI.
- *Matching gifts and corporate sponsorships.* Leveraging corporate donations and employer matching programs can boost revenue without increasing costs, thereby increasing ROI.
- *Volunteer involvement.* A strong volunteer network can reduce labor costs, thereby improving overall ROI. Well-trained volunteers help with donor outreach, thereby reducing the need for paid staff.

Pledge Fulfillment Rate

The pledge fulfillment rate is the percentage of pledged donations that are successfully collected by a nonprofit within a given timeframe. A high pledge fulfillment rate ensures that a nonprofit can count on pledged revenue, which reduces its financial uncertainty. The key factors influencing the pledge fulfillment rate are as follows:

- *Donor commitment.* Pledges made in emotional moments (e.g., at fundraising events) may not always translate into actual donations. In particular, first-time donors may be less likely to fulfill their pledges compared to long-term supporters.
- *Payment collection methods.* Automated payment options (credit cards, direct debit) increase fulfillment rates, while manual ones do not.

- *Follow-up communications.* Regular reminders (emails, phone calls, text messages) help donors remember their commitments.
- *Pledge duration.* Shorter pledge timelines (e.g., within six months) tend to have higher fulfillment rates. Also, installment plans (monthly, quarterly) improve retention compared to lump-sum payments.
- *Donor financial situations.* Economic downturns or personal financial hardships can lead to pledge cancellations or modifications. Offering flexible payment adjustments can help retain donors during these times.
- *Nonprofit credibility.* Organizations that consistently use funds effectively see higher pledge fulfillment.

Email/Direct Mail Response Rate

The email/direct response rate is a key metric that measures the percentage of recipients who take a desired action—such as making a donation, signing up for an event, or clicking on a call-to-action (CTA) - after receiving a nonprofit's fundraising email or direct mail appeal. A higher response rate suggests that a nonprofit's message resonates with donors and supporters, and helps nonprofits understand how well email and direct mail campaigns convert potential donors into actual contributors. The key factors influencing the email/direct response rate are as follows:

- *Audience segmentation.* Personalized emails targeted at specific donor groups (e.g., new donors vs. major donors) typically yield higher response rates than mass emails.
- *Compelling subject lines.* A strong, emotionally compelling subject line boosts open rates, which directly impacts response rates.
- *Call-to-action effectiveness.* The CTA should be clear, urgent, and easy to act upon (e.g., "Donate Now to Double Your Impact!).
- *Design and readability.* Mobile-friendly, scannable emails perform better. Direct mail should be visually appealing and easy to read, with a clear donation form.
- *Timing and frequency.* Emails sent mid-week (Tues-Thurs) and mid-morning (10 AM–Noon) generally perform best. Over-sending can lead to donor fatigue and unsubscribes, while under-sending may reduce engagement.
- *Follow-up.* Sending reminder emails to non-responders can boost response rates.

Online and Digital Engagement Metrics

There are several metrics associated with online and digital donor engagement, focusing on the online donation conversion rate, email open and click rates, and peer-to-peer fundraising comparisons. The key factors associated with each one are described next.

Online Donation Conversion Rate

The online donation conversion rate is a crucial metric for nonprofits, measuring the percentage of website visitors who complete a donation. A high online donation conversion rate means your website is effectively persuading visitors to give, while a low rate indicates potential barriers in the user experience. More conversions mean more funds raised without increasing traffic acquisition costs. The key factors influencing the online donation conversion rate are as follows:

- *Website design.* A cluttered or confusing donation page reduces conversions, while a simple, mobile-friendly, and visually appealing page increases trust and ease of use.
- *Page load speed.* Slow-loading pages cause visitors to abandon the process.
- *Clear and compelling call-to-action.* Generic CTAs like *"Click Here"* are less effective than *"Make a Difference – Donate Now"*. The CTA should be visible, emotionally compelling, and action-oriented.
- *Multiple payment options.* Offering credit/debit cards, PayPal, Apple Pay, Venmo, Google Pay, and ACH transfers increases accessibility. Many donors abandon donations if their preferred method isn't available.
- *Suggested giving levels.* Pre-set donation amounts (e.g., $25, $50, $100) help donors to decide quickly. A monthly giving option encourages recurring donations and increases the lifetime value of a donor.
- *Mobile optimization.* Since 50-60% of nonprofit website traffic comes from mobile devices, ensuring a mobile-friendly donation page is essential. Use large buttons, easy navigation, and a short, simple form for mobile users.
- *Urgency message.* Recent donor activity ("John from NY just donated!") creates a bandwagon effect. Also, limited-time matching campaigns or urgent appeals increase motivation.

Email Open and Click Rates

Email marketing is one of the most effective tools for nonprofit fundraising, and tracking email open and click rates is crucial for evaluating the success of your campaigns. These metrics help determine how well your emails are engaging supporters and whether your messaging is driving action. A high open rate suggests that your audience finds your emails relevant, while a strong click rate indicates that recipients are interested enough to take action. The key factors influencing open and click rates are as follows:

- *Compelling subject line.* A compelling subject line increases the likelihood of an email being opened. Keep it short, clear, and action-oriented (e.g., "Your Gift Can Save a Life Today" vs. "End-of-Year Fundraising Appeal").
- *Recognized sender name.* People are more likely to open emails from a sender they recognize and trust. Use a real person's name (e.g., "Sarah from [Nonprofit Name]") instead of a generic email address.
- *Personalization.* Emails addressed to recipients by name and tailored to their giving history or interests tend to perform better.

- *Segmentation*. Segmenting lists based on donor type (e.g., first-time vs. recurring donors) tends to improve engagement.
- *Timing and frequency*. Sending emails at optimal times (e.g., Tuesday or Thursday mornings) can boost open rates. Too many emails can lead to unsubscribes, while too few may reduce donor engagement.
- *Optimize for mobile*. Emails with a mobile-friendly design (clear fonts, single-column layout, and large buttons) have higher engagement.
- *Clear call-to-action*. The CTA should be bold, concise, and easy to find (e.g., "Donate Now," "Sign the Petition"). Emails with multiple CTAs can be overwhelming—one primary CTA works best.
- *Compelling content*. Emotionally driven storytelling, impact updates, and visuals (like donor testimonials and success stories) make emails more engaging and increase click-through rates.

Peer-to-Peer Fundraising Comparison

Peer-to-peer (P2P) fundraising is a powerful strategy where supporters raise money on behalf of a nonprofit by leveraging their personal networks. This metric measures how well different P2P campaigns or fundraisers perform relative to each other. By comparing P2P campaigns, nonprofits can identify which approaches yield the best results and thereby refine their future efforts. Also, understanding which fundraisers or teams are most effective helps in providing targeted support and recognition. The key factors influencing peer-to-peer fundraising performance are as follows:

- *Fundraiser engagement*. The most successful fundraisers are passionate advocates for the cause. Also, incentives, recognition, and gamification (e.g., leaderboards, badges) can boost motivation.
- *Fundraiser network size*. Individuals with larger or more engaged social circles tend to raise more.
- *Campaign duration*. Shorter campaigns (e.g., Giving Tuesday) create urgency, while longer campaigns allow sustained engagement.
- *Marketing support*. Providing fundraisers with templates, messaging, and graphics increases success, as well as regular check-ins and encouragement by the nonprofit staff.
- *Matching gifts*. Matching donation opportunities encourage larger contributions from donors.

Grant and Corporate Giving Metrics

There are several metrics associated with grants and corporate giving, focusing on the grant success rate and corporate sponsorship revenue. The key factors associated with each one are described next.

Grant Success Rate

The grant success rate is the percentage of grant applications submitted by a nonprofit that result in funding. A high success rate indicates that a nonprofit is targeting the right funders and submitting strong proposals, while a low rate may suggest the need for strategy adjustments. Grant writing requires significant time and effort. Tracking success rates helps nonprofits determine if resources are being used effectively or if efforts should be redirected to different funding opportunities. The key factors influencing the grant success rate are as follows:

- *Quality of proposals*. Well-researched, compelling, and data-driven proposals have higher chances of success. Also, experienced grant writers can significantly increase the quality of proposals. Investing in professional grant writers or training staff can improve success rates.
- *Funders' alignment with mission*. Nonprofits that apply to funders whose missions align closely with their programs are more likely to be awarded grants. Therefore, researching funders thoroughly before applying improves targeting efficiency.
- *Compliance*. Meeting all eligibility requirements avoids automatic disqualifications.
- *Relationship with grantors*. Nonprofits that build relationships with funders (through networking, meetings, and previous smaller grants) tend to have a better success rate.
- *Follow-up*. Engaging with funders before and after submission (e.g., requesting feedback on rejected proposals) increases the likelihood of future success.

Corporate Sponsorship Revenue

Corporate sponsorship revenue refers to the total financial contributions a nonprofit receives from businesses in exchange for brand visibility, recognition, or alignment with a charitable cause. These contributions can take various forms, including direct financial sponsorships, in-kind donations, or cause-marketing partnerships. These arrangements reduce a nonprofit's reliance on individual donations and grants and provides predictable revenue streams, especially through long-term partnerships. Furthermore, associations with reputable companies can enhance a nonprofit's visibility and trustworthiness. The key factors influencing corporate sponsorship revenue are as follows:

- *Alignment with corporate values*. Businesses are more likely to sponsor nonprofits whose mission aligns with their corporate social responsibility goals. For example, a health-focused nonprofit may secure a sponsorship from a pharmaceutical company.
- *Benefits for the sponsor*. Companies look for marketing value, such as logo placement, event sponsorships, or social media recognition. Thus, high-visibility opportunities (e.g., major events, media coverage) can attract larger sponsorship deals.

- *Strength of existing relationships*. Nonprofits with strong business networks or board members who have corporate connections are more successful in securing sponsorships.
- *Event success*. The effectiveness of fundraising events and campaigns directly impacts sponsorship revenue. Thus, higher attendance, media coverage, and engagement make sponsorships more appealing for corporations.
- *Economic conditions*. Sponsorship funding depends on corporate budgets, which may be influenced by economic conditions. In times of economic downturn, companies may reduce their sponsorship spending.
- *Engagement.* Effective follow-up, appreciation, and reporting to corporate sponsors encourage long-term support.

Summary

This chapter explored key revenue and donor metrics that are essential for nonprofit organizations to assess their financial health and fundraising effectiveness. It highlighted the importance of tracking total funds raised, revenue growth rate, average gift size, and recurring donation revenue while emphasizing donor retention, acquisition costs, and lifetime value. Additionally, the chapter discussed the significance of fundraising campaign metrics, online engagement, and corporate giving to enhance overall fundraising strategies. By monitoring these critical metrics, nonprofits can optimize their efforts, improve donor relationships, and ensure their long-term financial sustainability.

Chapter 10
Fundraising Best Practices

Introduction

Fundraising is essential for a nonprofit's financial sustainability and ability to achieve its mission. To maximize fundraising success, organizations should implement strategic approaches that engage donors, build trust, and diversify their revenue streams. Below are many best practices that can help nonprofits improve their fundraising efforts.

Strategic Planning and Goal Setting

1. *Set clear fundraising goals.* Define specific, measurable, achievable, relevant, and time-bound goals for each fundraising campaign. Having clear targets helps track progress and adjust strategies as needed.
2. *Develop a comprehensive fundraising plan.* Create a detailed plan that outlines fundraising activities, key dates, target audiences, and revenue projections. A well-structured plan keeps the team focused and accountable.
3. *Diversify revenue streams.* Relying on a single funding source is risky; nonprofits should seek multiple revenue streams, including grants, major donors, events, corporate sponsorships, and peer-to-peer fundraising. Diversification increases financial stability and reduces dependency on any one donor.
4. *Know your donor base.* Analyze donor demographics, giving patterns, and motivations to tailor fundraising appeals. Understanding what drives donations enables more personalized and effective engagement.
5. *Align fundraising with mission and impact.* Ensure fundraising campaigns clearly communicate how donations support the nonprofit's mission. Donors are more likely to give when they understand the tangible impact of their contributions.

Donor Engagement and Relationship Building

6. *Build long-term donor relationships.* Cultivate lasting relationships by consistently engaging with donors, not just when asking for money. Send updates, invite them to events, and show appreciation for their support.
7. *Segment donor communications.* Divide donors into categories based on giving history, interests, or engagement level. Personalized messaging increases donor retention and strengthens connections.
8. *Implement a donor stewardship program.* A structured stewardship program ensures donors feel valued through thank-you notes, phone calls, exclusive updates, and special recognition. Stewardship enhances donor loyalty and future giving.

9. *Offer monthly giving options.* Encouraging recurring donations provides a steady and predictable revenue stream. Subscription-based giving also deepens donor commitment to the nonprofit's mission.

10. *Host exclusive donor appreciation events.* Organizing special events for major donors, such as private dinners or behind-the-scenes tours, strengthens relationships and fosters deeper engagement. Personalized experiences increase donor retention.

Storytelling and Impact Communication

11. *Use impactful storytelling.* Share compelling stories about beneficiaries to create an emotional connection with donors. Real-life examples make the nonprofit's mission more relatable and inspiring.

12. *Showcase donor impact.* Highlight how donations have made a difference through reports, videos, and testimonials. Demonstrating impact reinforces trust and encourages continued giving.

13. *Create high-quality visual content.* Use professional images, videos, and infographics to communicate the nonprofit's work. Visual storytelling enhances engagement and increases donation rates.

14. *Develop a strong case for support.* Clearly articulate why the nonprofit exists, the problem it addresses, and how donations help. A well-crafted case for support makes fundraising appeals more persuasive.

15. *Leverage social proof.* Share testimonials, donor lists, and funding milestones to build credibility. People are more likely to give when they see others supporting the cause.

Effective Fundraising Campaigns

16. *Run multi-channel fundraising campaigns.* Combine direct mail, email, social media, and events to maximize reach and engagement. A diversified approach ensures broader donor participation.

17. *Use matching gift campaigns.* Encourage donors to take advantage of employer matching gift programs to double their contributions. Promoting matching gifts increases total funds raised.

18. *Host peer-to-peer fundraising campaigns.* Empower supporters to fundraise on behalf of the nonprofit by creating personal fundraising pages. Peer-to-peer campaigns expand the donor base and amplify impact.

19. *Launch limited-time giving challenges.* Time-sensitive campaigns, such as Giving Tuesday or 24-hour donation drives, create urgency and encourage immediate contributions. Short campaigns often lead to higher participation.

20. *Leverage crowdfunding platforms.* Use online crowdfunding tools like GoFundMe, Classy, or Mightycause to reach new donors. Crowdfunding campaigns work best when paired with compelling storytelling and social media promotion.

Optimizing Online Fundraising

21. *Have a mobile-friendly donation page.* Ensure that the donation page is easy to navigate on smartphones and tablets. Mobile-optimized pages increase conversion rates.
22. *Offer multiple payment options.* Allow donors to give via credit card, PayPal, Venmo, and cryptocurrency. More payment choices improve accessibility and convenience.
23. *Use an easy-to-remember donation link.* Create a short, branded URL for the donation page to simplify giving. Simple links increase the likelihood of donations.
24. *Implement a one-click donation option.* Reduce friction in the donation process by enabling one-click giving for returning donors. A seamless process encourages repeat contributions.
25. *Personalize online giving experiences.* Address donors by name and offer customized donation suggestions based on their past giving behavior. Personalization enhances engagement and generosity.

Event-Based Fundraising Strategies

26. *Host annual signature fundraising events.* Establishing a recurring event, such as a gala, auction, or charity run, builds tradition and donor loyalty. Signature events become reliable revenue sources.
27. *Incorporate virtual fundraising events.* Online events, such as virtual concerts, webinars, or live-streamed auctions, expand donor reach. Virtual fundraising reduces logistical costs and increases accessibility.
28. *Offer VIP experiences for major donors.* Providing exclusive perks, such as private meetings with leadership or premium event seating, enhances donor engagement and giving levels.
29. *Maximize sponsorship opportunities.* Secure corporate sponsorships for fundraising events to cover costs and boost revenue. Sponsors benefit from brand exposure and social impact.
30. *Sell branded merchandise.* Offering T-shirts, tote bags, or mugs as part of fundraising events creates an additional revenue stream and promotes brand awareness.

Corporate and Community Partnerships

31. *Develop corporate giving programs.* Encourage businesses to support the nonprofit through workplace giving, employee donation matching, or corporate grants. Corporate partnerships increase funding opportunities.
32. *Engage local businesses in fundraising campaigns.* Partner with restaurants, retail stores, or service providers that donate a percentage of sales. Community partnerships boost revenue and visibility.
33. *Leverage board member networks for fundraising.* Encourage board members to use their personal and professional networks to secure donations. Board involvement strengthens credibility and financial support.

34. *Encourage employee giving programs.* Partner with companies that offer payroll giving or volunteer grant programs. Workplace giving simplifies donations and fosters long-term support.
35. *Host collaborative fundraisers with other nonprofits.* Joint fundraising events increase outreach and share costs. Partnering with aligned organizations strengthens a nonprofit's impact and credibility.

Ongoing Evaluation and Improvement

36. *Track fundraising metrics and KPIs.* Monitor donor retention rates, average gift sizes, and campaign ROI to evaluate success. Data-driven insights guide future fundraising strategies.
37. *Solicit feedback from donors.* Conduct surveys to understand donor preferences and improve future campaigns. Listening to supporters enhances engagement and retention.
38. *A/B test fundraising appeals.* Experiment with different messaging, visuals, and calls to action to determine what resonates best with donors. Testing improves conversion rates.
39. *Update fundraising strategies annually.* Review the organization's past performance and adjust strategies based on changing donor behaviors and trends. Continuous improvement ensures long-term success.
40. *Celebrate fundraising milestones.* Acknowledge campaign achievements publicly to inspire further giving. Recognition builds momentum and encourages future contributions by donors.

Summary

By implementing these best practices, nonprofits can enhance their fundraising effectiveness, build stronger donor relationships, and create sustainable financial growth. Successful fundraising requires a combination of strategy, engagement, innovation, and continuous evaluation. By staying adaptable and leveraging multiple fundraising channels, nonprofits can increase their impact and secure the resources needed to fulfill their missions.

Glossary

A

A/B test. A marketing strategy in which two versions of a digital asset (like a webpage, ad, or email) are tested to determine which performs better based on key metrics like conversion rates.

B

Bequest. A gift made through a donor's will or estate plan, allowing them to leave assets, money, or property to a nonprofit organization after their passing.

D

Direct response fundraising. A strategy used by nonprofits to solicit donations from individual donors through direct and measurable channels—such as mail, email, digital ads, or telemarketing—designed to prompt an immediate response.

Donor pyramid. A visual representation of a nonprofit's donor base, illustrating the progression from lower-level donors at the bottom to major and legacy donors at the top.

Donor value. The total benefit a donor provides to a nonprofit organization over the lifetime of their engagement, typically measured in financial contributions, loyalty, advocacy, and personal involvement.

E

Empathy. The ability to understand and share the feelings, thoughts, and experiences of another person from their perspective.

F

Foundation. A nonprofit organization that provides funding and support to charitable causes, typically through grants and endowments, to advance its philanthropic mission.

Fundraising. The process of collecting voluntary financial contributions or resources from individuals or organizations to support a cause, project, or organization.

I

In-memory giving. A type of charitable donation made to honor and commemorate a deceased loved one, often supporting a cause that was meaningful to them.

P

Planned giving. A strategic way for nonprofit donors to contribute future gifts through wills, trusts, annuities, or other financial instruments to support a charitable organization's long-term mission.

S

Stewardship. The ethical and intentional management of donor relationships through appreciation, transparency, and accountability to foster trust and long-term support.

W

Warm glow effect. The emotional satisfaction that individuals experience when they engage in prosocial behavior, such as charitable giving, regardless of the actual impact of their actions.

Index